What Others Say About William (Bill) H. McGill Jr. and *Relentless Caring* . . .

"Bill McGill is a true visionary who has literally transformed an industry with his entrepreneurial mindset, relentless pursuit of innovation, and true understanding of the importance of every person. He is a thought leader who cares, who listens, and who everyone knows and respects. This doesn't come from words—it comes from action and from integrity. As someone who teaches entrepreneurship, I have been incredibly impressed with Bill's ability to see opportunity and to execute through others. He truly leads from the heart."

—Rebecca J. White, PhD, Author, *See, Do Repeat*, and James W. Walter Distinguished Chair of Entrepreneurship, University of Tampa, and Director, John P. Lowth Center for Entrepreneurship

"Culture is the heartbeat of any successful company or organization. Bill McGill expresses the meaning of culture in two words: relentless caring! This book is a must-read for anyone who cares about building a 'family team' of leaders with common values, constancy of purpose, and continued process improvement. It's a never-ending commitment to mentoring, motivating, listening, and leading people. *Relentless Caring* is the blueprint of how Bill started a company and over time built it into a $2 billion conglomerate that amazingly maintains the integrity and values of a family thanks to his relentless caring."

—Dick Lazzara, Principal, Lazzara Creative, and former President and Designer, Lazzara Yacht Corporation

"*Relentless Caring* is in part an MBA manual that shows how sincere caring can turbo-boost all leadership methods. Bill uses his experiences, peppered with quotes by famous people, to teach how sincere caring can make leadership skills more effective—from listening, hiring, and firing to coaching, compensation, benefits, goal setting, accountability, and even organizing one's day. Further, he debunks the 'realistic' practices by public companies like chasing stock price, cutting back on customer service, and keeping healthcare costs down by cutting coverage to the bone."

—Bradford D. Smart, PhD, Author, the Topgrading series and *Foolproof Hiring*

"Every business is reliant on the people we hire, train, and mentor. A business grows, succeeds, or fails because of the people, and the ability to maximize their growth, personally and professionally. Bill McGill has been masterful in recognizing and delivering on the art of relentless caring. In this book, Bill delivers his message in an easily readable, understandable, and achievable format. Bill's message is timeless yet easy to overlook as a business grows and expands. Bill and his team built MarineMax into the world leader of boating and yachting, an incredible company with an ethos and culture that values people and their growth and success as well as doing good business. Bill's innate entrepreneurial spirit, his investment in excellent teammates, diligence, and integrity have proven to be incredibly successful, radically changing and improving the yachting and boating industry, and building MarineMax into the world leader of the marine industry."

—Kevin Merrigan, Chairman, Northrop & Johnson Yacht Brokerage

RELENTLESS CARING

If You Don't Give a Damn, Don't Expect Anyone Else To

William H. McGill Jr.

MATT HOLT

Matt Holt Books
An Imprint of BenBella Books, Inc.
Dallas, TX

Matt Holt is an imprint of BenBella Books, Inc.
10440 N. Central Expressway
Suite 800
Dallas, TX 75231
benbellabooks.com
Send feedback to feedback@benbellabooks.com

BenBella and *Matt Holt* are federally registered trademarks.

Printed in the United States of America
10 9 8 7 6 5 4 3 2 1

Library of Congress Control Number: 2023030520
ISBN 9781637744727 (hardcover)
ISBN 9781637744734 (electronic)

Copyediting by Alyn Wallace
Proofreading by Lisa Story and Michael Fedison
Text design and composition by Jordan Koluch
Cover design by Brigid Pearson
Printed by Lake Book Manufacturing

To the MarineMax team for all their contributions, guidance, and friendship,
as well as the strong culture we have created together.
And to my wife, Irina, and my family for always being there for me.

Contents

Foreword

These days almost every CEO talks about the importance of caring. But it is the rare leader who relentlessly puts people first over fast profits and creates a successful company in the process.

Bill McGill is that leader. He cares, and he demonstrates it every day. He never waivers.

Unlike most company leaders, Bill doesn't chase quarterly financial reports or one-and-done sales. Instead he promises to be there for his team and his customers for the long haul . . . and he is.

I have had the opportunity—and privilege—to see Bill in action as a leader for years. In fact, I admired Bill's leadership and approach to business so much that, in 2021, I joined the board of directors of the company he founded—MarineMax—and now serve as chairman of the board.

What differentiates Bill as a business leader is that he knows his values—they do not change; he instinctively knows what is right and follows through. He makes the process of filtering and finding rarefied talent seem simple. It is not. He's a master at managing and leading, and understands that one of the greatest luxuries of a leader today is the absence of worry.

Bill created a MarineMax culture where his teams are motivated to teach and serve others—a culture of relentless caring. He shows us how the right balance of real leadership and genuine caring can lead to long-term success.

Now Bill shares that wisdom in these pages. Lucky for us.

Adam Johnson,
Chairman and CEO of NetJets Inc.,
a Berkshire Hathaway company

Introduction

When was the last time you encountered a manager or an organization that first and foremost relentlessly cared about you and your family? If you're fortunate enough to have encountered that person or done business with a company like that—no matter its size, industry, or if it was public or private—chances are you've returned again and again and recommended them to others.

Get ready for a unique, yet powerful approach to business success, a way to do business that's simple to implement and doesn't require a huge up-front investment, but routinely pays dividends again and again. That's because relentless caring creates strong loyalties despite the state of the economy or circumstances. This loyalty exists both internally with your teams and externally with your customers. It's loyalty that translates into dedicated employees and repeat customers, crucial elements for success in today's highly competitive markets.

This is a different kind of leadership that starts with caring about others. This isn't just talking about caring or tossing around inspirational quotes. This is relentless caring given freely inside and outside an organization.

As an entrepreneur, engineer, efficiency expert, and executive chairman of the board of MarineMax (NYSE-HZO), I, along with MarineMax's team, know relentless caring works. That approach helped transform our company from a small group of disparate boat retailers into the world's largest marine conglomerate with more than two million customers—and upended an industry in the process.

Today's MarineMax facilities in Fort Myers, Florida, shown in the two photos above.

Mainstream commercial marine retailing used to revolve around the "push" model: manufacturers and dealers built a product, pushed it out to retailers, and expected them to sell it to consumers. But we at MarineMax had other ideas. Committed to customer service and caring beyond expectations, we embraced a model that focused on giving customers what they wanted and developed the "pull" model for marine sales. Now customers' needs and wants take precedence over mass sales of the same product. This is personalization front and center—relentless caring applied to marine manufacturing, sales, and service.

That's what I refer to as managing from the heart instead of only focusing on the balance sheet; it's leadership with the long-term view rather than simply pursuit of short-term profits. Combine that foundation with a passion for what you are doing along with certain essential tenets for doing business where you keep other people's well-being in mind, and success is inevitable no matter the industry—and in good times and bad.

In *Relentless Caring*, I share what it takes in business to truly care about others 24/7 and generate solid profits at the same time. You will learn why having the right people in the right jobs matters and how to identify and take care of those people and their families; why persistence, consistency, and risk are essential to success; and why investing in basic tools like personality profiling and a structured hiring and promotion system contributes to an organization making the right decisions to be winners instead of those who come up short.

This isn't a book that relies on buzzwords like "servant leadership," "giveback," "corporate culture," "employee engagement," "work-life balance," "ideation," "collaboration," "customer relationship management," or any of the other myriad hot topics of discussion these days. This isn't about giving team members a free day to volunteer at their charity of choice, either, or occasionally taking the gang out for happy hour or a company picnic.

This is a step-by-step playbook for leaders on how to genuinely deliver goodness and kindness in the business world day in and day out, to do so tirelessly across all aspects of an organization—internally with workers and externally with customers—and to grow profits.

I started with one small boat dealership in St. Petersburg, Florida. Eventually I partnered with four other retail boat dealers, and from there we built MarineMax into a more than $2 billion global conglomerate. We sell small and large boats, build boats, service boats, and deliver well beyond the expectations of our customers. That's not myth; that's reality with the numbers to prove it.

No matter how large or small your organization, relentless caring causes people to want to work with you and for you, and customers to become like family. As a young engineer working with NASA, I learned that firsthand.

As workforces, workplaces, and consumer tastes and demands evolve, that kind of caring is fast becoming table stakes, whether you're running a small mom-and-pop shop, a global conglomerate, or something in between. Where once cut-rate prices, impersonal self-service, and mass sale-a-thons propelled the sales leaders, tomorrow's consumers—workers and customers—expect personalization, caring, ease of experience, fair pricing, and services far beyond expectations. Genuine and selfless caring delivers all that and more.

Relentless Caring shows you how to do the right thing and explores why some companies and leaders fall short. Other topics addressed in the book include:

- why certain actions convey sincere caring and others miss the mark;

- tips and proven guidance for how to build a strong caring culture that won't erode the bottom line (of note: it's about repetition to create habits that eventually become part of an organization's culture);
- why most would-be leaders fall short with their leadership;
- how to embrace problems to capitalize on opportunities;
- how and why risk is an essential element for growth; and
- how to take the right risks for optimal gain.

Throughout the book there also will be a series of "Assess Your Leadership" questions and answers to help you and your company get on the relentless caring track and stay there. The end of each chapter includes a roundup of the key points in the chapter.

Some people may consider my ideas too simple or my approach nothing new. But even in tough times, my approach has proven successful as other people and their companies struggle. That suggests that just because we've heard something before doesn't mean we've yet learned how to embrace it and make it an integral part of doing business.

The experiences, wisdom, and real stories shared in these pages can be the game changer.

Part I

SUCCESS IS UP TO YOU

Chapter One

Why Care?

When your neighbor's tractor gets stuck in the ditch,
better stop to help him because the next tractor
that gets stuck likely will be yours.

—AN EARLY LESSON FROM LIFE ON THE FARM

Relentless caring makes the difference between success and failure in good times and bad. Caring spans generations and job titles, industries and organizations. It isn't difficult or expensive, but it does require conscious effort and the right mindset.

Can't-be-bothered-by-you, too-busy, or I'm-the-boss attitudes don't cut it. Neither does saying one thing and doing another, whether we're talking about your teams or your customers.

Even a small gesture of concern for the well-being of others—going out of your way to help someone or ask about their family, for example—can make a huge difference. It's such a simple approach to doing business, yet it's regularly ignored or overlooked.

A POWERFUL LESSON

I first learned about the power of relentless caring as an aerospace engineer working with Northrop Nortronics as a contractor on NASA's Space Station Chamber at Langley Air Force Base in Virginia. We were conducting tests and evaluating life-support equipment for what then was a future long-term space station. I was a lead engineer and excited about the potential to be on track for the first team that would man such a station.

Among the simulations we did were twenty-eight-day stints with a team of four inside a twenty-five-foot-diameter, reduced-pressure simulation chamber. Needless to say, it was close quarters (see photo). I was included in many of the tests. Scientific experts monitored life-support conditions inside the sealed chamber, and after each test, psychologists evaluated the effects of this unique form of isolation on each of us as individuals.

We had no choice but to work as a team—the four of us inside the cramped two-level chamber as well as the support team outside. Our only communication twenty-four hours a day was with a team of external scientists and experts. As part of the tests, we were prohibited from communicating with anyone but the support team. That meant we were cut off from the outside world, including our families. That was a way to keep the team inside focused on the life-support efforts and not family at home or other distractions.

The author in full spacesuit garb as an aerospace engineer working as a contractor with Northrop Nortronics on NASA's Space Station Chamber at Langley Air Force Base in Virginia.

I quickly realized that no matter the situation, caring was the differentiator. That was a lesson I also learned growing up on a farm in Tennessee where sometimes your neighbors were a lifeline if a tractor broke down or crops had to come out of the field before an impending storm. Everyone had to care about everyone else because the success of the tests and the safety of those of us in the chamber depended on it.

When the support team called in to the "station," I made a point to always ask how they *and* their families were doing. This wasn't idle chitchat, but rather true and genuine concern for others. My colleagues understood my sincerity, knew I cared, and that I wanted to help in any way possible. When a problem surfaced, we solved it together and looked for opportunities to learn and improve.

These unusual confines led to another revelation for me. Sometimes individuals designated as team "leaders" don't truly care about others and as a result can't lead successfully when confronted with leadership responsibilities. More than once inside the chamber, in the face of a life-and-death decision, the designated leader froze and couldn't make the decisions necessary to ensure the safety of the team.

Those tests may have been part of a multibillion-dollar NASA program, but leaders who don't sincerely care or can't lead is a too-familiar scenario in all kinds of organizations. Real leaders show their teams they care with their actions, whether those are teams of technicians, top executives, line workers, or all of the above.

I remember an incident from those early days with NASA when there was a problem with one of the electrolysis units that generate the oxygen the team breathes inside the chamber. In other words, it was an emergency. The team leader at the time was a well-credentialed engineer who panicked and couldn't lead under pressure. Instead, a low-level technician had to take control and direct others to do what was necessary to bring in external oxygen to save the participants' lives.

MANAGING FROM THE HEART

Caring for your team as employees is one thing, but caring for their families, too, demonstrates that caring is more than a business management word. Whenever our company—MarineMax (NYSE: HZO)—acquires a business, standard operating procedure is to sit down with the company's managers and leadership to discuss MarineMax's culture and commitment to relentless caring.

Not long ago we purchased a yacht manufacturer in the Midwest. Even though this was a solid company that produced quality products, it was clear that an ultra-focus on relentlessly caring about others—what I often refer to as managing from the heart—wasn't the modus operandi. We weren't looking to dramatically change the company's culture overnight, in part because our experiences have taught us that simply isn't realistic. Instead, we believed that, with our guidance, the manufacturer would increase its focus on its teams (and customers), and hence its culture would begin to change. Success in transforming a culture, after all, is about laying out a goal (in this case, relentless caring), and passionately and repeatedly reinforcing the goal through actions to create new habits, which eventually lead to changing a culture.

Standard practice for most organizations instead is to present the goal with little or no input from stakeholders and expect their teams to accept those goals. The goal then becomes a dictum rather than an action that, when repeated, becomes habit and eventually part of the organization's culture. A dictum is not the way for something to become a natural action and part of a culture.

To encourage an attitude of greater caring, a supervisor could, for example, show up across various shifts and take the time to engage workers. That simple gesture of presence can make a big difference. Something else that reflects caring is regularly scheduled meetings—virtual and in person. I'm sure plenty of people question the idea of more meetings as a symbol of caring. But when meetings are held for the right reasons and are respectful of participants' obligations, they convey that a person/company cares about their teams. With any initiative, sincerity *and* substance are essential.

Without this kind of interaction and civility, a leader risks sending their team the message that they just don't care about them. And guess what? If you don't care about your team, don't expect your team to care about you, your customers, or the company. Instead of a well-oiled, top-producing manufacturing line of dedicated team members or a well-connected collaborative team of people working in person, remotely, or a combination of both, you'll end up with something far less positive and certainly not sustainable.

TRANSFORMING YOUR ORGANIZATION'S CULTURE

Goal→Repetition→Habit→Culture

1. Believe in and explain the goal to your teams; make sure it's clear and that expectations are understood and achievable.
2. Repeat the goal verbally and through your actions again and again and again.
3. Repeat No. 2 until the behavior becomes habit.
4. Habit eventually leads to a culture change.
5. Celebrate everyone who made it happen.
6. Continue to reinforce the culture through repetition, discussion, and your actions.

When we met with team members at the yacht manufacturer, we didn't offer shallow words and repeat tired promises. We asked questions about important plant and company issues, listened to everyone's answers, and followed up to make sure we acted on the discussions. We worked hard to connect with people individually by asking about their families, what they enjoyed doing for entertainment, their hobbies, and more.

As a result of our personalized caring, the manufacturer's team began to share with us what they thought were the company's strengths and weaknesses and possible ways to improve.

This wasn't a one-and-done visit; this was connecting. We continued working with, listening to, and talking to both the company's leadership and teams. We began with the company's president, showing by example how to interact with team members. (Today he's doing an incredible job. Best of all, he enjoys managing, walking around, and showing the team he truly cares.) Over time, senior managers recognized we were serious about our goal to create a caring culture, and they understood the impact of connecting with their teams not only in their jobs but also personally.

And guess what? We began to see a change in the overall attitude of team members. Instead of "employees" producing a product and doing the minimum required (oftentimes less), morale, plant production, and product quality excelled. Within a year, the company's revenues and profits increased dramatically. Suggestions for new and better ways to do things began to bubble up from team members across the board as they saw managers spending less time in their offices and more time interacting with—and caring about—workers.

Such is the power of relentless caring.

MAKING RELENTLESS CARING REAL

Today plenty of people and leaders in the workplace claim they care, but not enough actually do. Look through job search listings and it seems like everyone touts their great caring culture. "Giveback" is a big buzzword. Talk about honesty, integrity, diversity, fairness, and work-life balance is trendy too. But not many leaders—and, as an extension, their companies—practice relentless caring.

Relentless caring is more than occasionally asking about someone's family or giving your team members a day off. It's not espousing the importance of work-life balance—then demanding your teams work nights and weekends or overloading them with goals or work that you know cannot realistically be accommodated during a regular workweek.

Relentless caring is a 24/7 commitment that nets never-ending positive results. Those results include team members who are empowered and thus willing to *always* do the right thing for customers no matter the situation. It also means customers for life as well as unsolicited referrals.

An easy example of when we experience an organization walking the talk or not about caring is airline travel. COVID-19 pandemic-related excuses aside, experiences vary vastly across different airlines. Most, if not all, U.S. airlines advertise their caring customer service. But few truly and consistently deliver.

With MarineMax's more than one hundred locations across the country and around the globe, I have spent plenty of time on airplanes. That traveling has taught me firsthand that one airline—for me it's Delta—will bend over backward to accommodate issues with flight changes and personal customer needs. That compares with another airline, no names mentioned, that makes last-minute changes and leaves its customers, myself included, forced to fend for themselves.

All of us, too, likely have experienced a retailer—virtual or otherwise—that treats its customers respectfully, responds quickly to concerns, and provides easy, smooth returns. We've also dealt with one that's the opposite. Chances are customers of the former will return, while the latter will go elsewhere and share the shortcomings with others. Caring is the differentiator.

Consider how true caring translates into everyday actions. One of our customers called his MarineMax dealership on a Friday afternoon with boat troubles that threatened a planned weekend on the water with family and friends. The man tried, but he couldn't clearly explain the problem with his boat to the MarineMax service adviser. So, after the service adviser finished work that day, he went out to the customer's boat to figure out the exact problem. No one told the adviser to do that; he just did it. Then, later that evening a technician went out to the boat and made the necessary repairs so that it was ready for the customer's Saturday's morning excursion with his family and friends.

That's relentless caring about customers. And that brings those customers back again and again, and they share their positive experiences with their friends.

COMMUNICATION AND CONNECTION

If relentless caring is such a no-brainer, it would make sense that everyone engages in it. But practically speaking, it's not quite that simple. Like any skill, relentless caring takes commitment and practice to master.

Caring about both your customers and your teams requires powerful communication that includes:

- talking *and* listening
- living your values and the values of your company
- accountability
- persistence
- follow-through

With your teams, powerful communication includes:

- active listening
- honesty
- rewards and recognition
- providing equitable remuneration and promotions
- quality healthcare
- developing career tracks
- guidance and direction
- friendship
- caring

When it comes to your customers, it's about honesty, too, as well as much more, including:

- listening
- caring
- fair pricing
- friendship
- guidance
- kindness
- service beyond expectations
- exceptional-quality care

That's a lot to demand, and we'll examine each of these more closely in this book.

But first things first. Relentless caring starts with asking questions, listening to the answers, and following up—internally with your teams and externally with your customers. This kind of connected communication is especially important as workplaces and spaces evolve. Whether your company is a large manufacturer, a small retailer, a midsize service provider operating remotely, or some other type of business, it's critical to learn to make the time to ask all stakeholders simple questions that demonstrate that you care.

Here are a few of the questions I like to use to help connect with others, whether team members or customers. They seem relatively benign and, again, like no-brainers, but they are essential to making connections:

- What do you like to do outside of the office?
- What do you and your family and friends do for fun?
- How large is your immediate family? (That's instead of asking, "Do you have kids?" which is a question that can sometimes lead to brief discomfort if the answer is "No.")
- How can we help you or your life be better? (Rather than respond sarcastically or with an unrealistic request, most people truly appreciate this kind of caring approach and welcome the opportunity to be heard.)
- Tell me about what I can do to make your job better. (People appreciate this too.)
- Are you having fun?

Crucial to any discission is genuinely listening to the other person, and then following up. This isn't about making anyone feel uncomfortable. It's not gratuitous actions or idle conversation, violating personal space or time, or being nosy or a busybody. This is making the effort to connect with people in a way that shows you care about them as individuals and fosters long-term connection and commitment.

Consider the tale of two very different managers. After NASA, I went to work for the Kendall Company as a manufacturing engineer at a plant in Franklin, Kentucky. Kendall was a leading maker of bandages, padding, and healthcare dressings under brands like Curad and Curity.

My job was to make sure the plant's machines were maintained and to improve them in order to bolster productivity. My job description as an engineer didn't say anything about morale or motivating the team, but I knew the power of caring as a catalyst to fuel productivity.

The production plant operated on three shifts including the overnight ("graveyard") shift. Anyone who has worked a graveyard shift knows that few, if any, senior leaders ever show up late at night or early in the morning, let alone go out of their way to bond with and motivate those overnight team members.

When I joined Kendall, I began to spend time on each of the three shifts to show team members they mattered and that I cared. The manager of the first and second shifts (I'll call him Sam) was surprised by my actions. No one had ever done that in his tenure with the company. His boss (and mine)—the plant's manager—only occasionally showed up on the factory floor, and when he did, it was primarily to demand unrealistic output goals. That senior manager never asked for suggestions from the frontline workers who understood the problems firsthand. I could easily see that his disregard for others was demoralizing the entire team.

I talked with Sam about how a true leader conveys they care through their actions. To prove that these weren't just hollow words, I modeled the behavior, showing up across the various shifts to talk with, encourage, and work alongside team members.

Even the smallest gestures of kindness make a big difference, and most importantly, let others know you care. For example, on one out-of-state business trip, I made a special stop at a country ham producer to negotiate a sizable discount for Kendall employees. This small detour cost only a few minutes of my time, but the Kendall team was absolutely thrilled to be able to buy their favorite hams at a discounted price. That may not seem like a big deal, but it meant a lot to my colleagues.

Sam began to embrace the idea of connecting with his team members too. He made sure to, periodically, be physically present across the shifts. He would show up at all hours, stop and talk with team members, and worked hard to develop friendships. Workers' attitudes on Sam's shifts soon improved, as did production and morale.

At the other end of the spectrum, I also tried to help the manager of the Kendall plant's graveyard shift understand the importance of a caring mindset. But he resisted. To this manager, the bottom line was about more production and less waste, whether time, product, or people. He insisted that he didn't need to get to know his team or even care about them. After all, they were paid for their work and should be thankful to have a job. That attitude eventually proved the manager's undoing. As production across Sam's shifts increased, it faltered on the graveyard shift and the manager was fired.

As an aside, many years later, long after I had left Kendall and Sam had earned a promotion to plant manager, our paths crossed again. My former colleague thanked me for my suggestions about the importance of caring and being present. The advice, he said, had served him well, not only throughout his career but also in his personal life.

TODAY'S SPECIAL CHALLENGE

These days with so many people working remotely and the primary form of communication being either the telephone, text, email, Zoom, or some other videoconferencing tool, connecting with your teams is a special challenge. But I believe from every problem can come opportunity if one just looks for it.

In this case the opportunities involve creating personal connections with your remote teams. Leaders and managers must make the extra effort to connect with off-site team members by offering accolades for performance, recognition of special times like birthdays and anniversaries, and check-ins about families and activities. Younger generations especially appreciate this kind of caring. (I'll talk more about this later.)

CARING FOR YOUR CUSTOMERS

Your teams remember caring and so do your customers. A customer never forgets—the good, the not so good, and especially the downright ugly. That's a guarantee regardless of the company, the leader, or the industry. It's also a strong incentive to pay attention to taking care of your customers and their families, not just before the sale, but long after as well.

At MarineMax, our team cares for our customers throughout and well beyond the purchase process. We teach buyers and their families/friends about the products they purchase, provide empathy during any service calls, and share with them ways to enjoy the boating lifestyle. That includes opportunities to join us for MarineMax Getaways!®, which are boat flotillas and trips we operate to various destinations where participants meet boating families and make new friendships.

Company performance, after all, isn't just about sales. In fact, sales numbers are only a small part of the equation and relying solely on them to measure performance is shortsighted.

Think about it: customer interaction and satisfaction can impact your bottom line so much more over the long haul because satisfied customers return to buy more, and they tell their friends—who in turn tell other friends. The result is a relatively low-cost cycle of repeat and referral business. That's why caring about and measuring customer satisfaction is crucial to growing any business long-term.

Companies, consultants, and self-described experts tout all kinds of tools, metrics, services, software, and more to determine success at customer satisfaction. Some approaches work; others not so much.

Today the MarineMax family numbers in the millions. These are team members and their families as well as current and past customers. We don't forget them and they don't forget us because, as is ingrained in our culture, we truly work hard to exceed their expectations for customer service.

Repeat customers make up more than 60 percent of our business in larger boats and yachts. That's a lot considering our customer database totals 2.4 million people, with almost half of those active customers. Those repeat customers don't just buy one more boat either. Some have bought as many as a dozen additional boats from us over the years. That's solid ROI—return on investment—from repeat sales, and it's just one part of MarineMax's growth strategy. Referral business from happy customers makes up another huge chunk.

All of this is a testament to our high level of customer satisfaction. That's because built into our company's culture is the concept of customer service that really does exceed expectations. We don't just talk about it; we actually achieve it. We determine our customers' level of satisfaction with who we are, how we interact, how we serve their needs (or don't) based on their feedback. That feedback is nonnegotiable and absolutely, unequivocally essential with every single customer interaction. Our teams review and discuss that customer feedback daily too.

Rather than look to complex metrics, algorithms, formulas, or personal interpretations for evaluating company performance, following any interaction with a customer we ask just two questions:

- How would you recommend our company to a friend or associate on a scale of 0 to 10, with 10 being the top score?
- Why did you give our company that score?

The formal approach we use to ask those questions and measure the response is based on the Net Promoter Score® (NPS). I first learned about NPS from the book *The Ultimate Question* by Fred Reichheld. Reichheld talks about how the true measure of customer satisfaction is not the typical customer satisfaction index (CSI), which is a series of questions that are often only answered as the result of a company begging, threatening, or bribing customers with cash/merchandise/discount incentives to get them to respond. (And yes, all that really happens.) We'll discuss NPS in more detail later in the book, but after nearly two decades of success with NPS, we at MarineMax consider it the gold standard and an accurate baseline to measure customer satisfaction with our team and company.

Whatever approach you and your organization use to measure customer satisfaction, it should be fair and consistent, and your company must be relentless in getting that honest feedback from everyone. There can't be payback for commenting—no freebies, no discounts, nothing to taint responses in any way.

SPECIAL CHALLENGES

The marine industry, like other industries, has its special challenges—everything from machinery breakdowns to extensive product repairs associated with a water environment to even the lack of skilled boat operators. That's why it's so important that we take care of customers. We don't just sell products: We guide. We train. We teach. We follow up. And we show our customers how to have fun.

Our approach (as should others' approaches) relies on a culture of relentless caring with a foundation that begins with our senior management and extends to all our teams. If the CEO and top management are not tuned in to relentless caring and demonstrating that caring to all, caring won't become a culture in an organization. We always let our teams know that we care about them so they in turn care about their customers.

Done right, relentless caring is a self-perpetuating cycle.

THE POWER OF WORDS

The words you use with your teams and your customers matter, too, because word choice reveals attitude. Words should be motivational and convey personalized respect and recognition. Your words communicate that you care (or don't care) about stakeholders, whether internally (team members) or externally (customers, investors). Often, leaders forget that.

Reflection of Reality

The above is another lesson I learned during my time in NASA's cramped space station chamber. The word "employee," for example, has no business in a workplace of any size. After all, back then and now, we all should be a team working together to accomplish a goal.

In the same vein, "headquarters" is an outdated and inaccurate term. Corporate or main offices exist to help their teams of workers. At MarineMax, we refer to our corporate office as "team support." The job of a headquarters, after all, is to facilitate the efforts of team members as they work with customers and each other.

Those revelations about terminology happened for me long before words like collaboration, and creativity, even company culture, were standard workplace vernacular. Back then in the workplace, for most, "collaboration" referred to doing exactly as the boss dictated and "creativity" meant figuring out a faster way to do the same thing, but only if the boss okayed it first.

And "communication" meant listening to the boss—definitely not questioning operations or looking for a better, faster way to achieve a goal. Though much has changed in the workplace today, unfortunately this practice still seems to persist because some organizations—and too many leaders—have failed to evolve and still treat team members as disposable underlings.

Before someone objects to or rolls their eyes at the importance of the right terminology in relation to relentless caring, think about this: A retailer without a sales team can't sell. A marketer without a marketing team is full of hot air. A manufacturer without a factory team can't manufacture much of anything. A caring work environment creates an atmosphere of compassion and fulfillment, which becomes contagious to customers and suppliers.

"Boss" is another word that requires a readjustment. We are a team that works together. The terminology to use instead of "I" is "we" because the goal is to make fellow team members as well as customers feel as if they are part of our family.

Empowering Your Teams

Especially when price is involved, we often hear salespeople say things like, "Let me check with the boss first." Or, if it's a manufacturer-related service issue, the common response from most is, "I will need to check with the manufacturer first."

However, in those same situations, a relentlessly caring approach means empowering your teams to offer instantaneous responses and solutions. The right response is: "Let me see what I can do to meet your need or concern because we value you as a customer and appreciate your business." Then, the customer / potential customer and the salespeople together solve the issue. Behind the scenes, often a manager or manufacturer also may need to be involved. If so, though, it's done quietly to help solve the problem. Customer satisfaction, not placing blame, is tantamount.

Using the right words is one thing; it's another to live them and teach others to choose their words carefully and use the right terminology. Also, when you as a leader are passionate about what you're doing and having fun doing it, it's contagious. Modeling the right behavior combined with ongoing repetition of the right words helps change behaviors. Once again, it's about creating new habits that eventually, when practiced enough, become standard procedure.

A little extra incentive can help convert people to new word usage too. When we started MarineMax, to encourage our people to use "team support" instead of "headquarters," anyone who referred to corporate as anything other than team support had to put $1 in a box. I think we only collected a few hundred dollars before everyone adjusted to the new terminology. Now, almost twenty-five years later, "team support" is an accepted part of our company's vernacular. If a new hire slips up and uses the wrong terminology, another team member will gently remind them of the right word choice.

"Love" Your Teams

Another popular workplace buzzword these days is *love*—managers and leaders are supposed to give their teams more love so they are more engaged and committed. This goes beyond simple respect to encompass genuine and passionate caring for team members as individuals. Some experts in part blame the Great Resignation—the post-COVID-19 wave of workers quitting their jobs—on a lack of love or appreciation shown to team members by employers.[1]

This isn't romantic love, of course, and this isn't a new idea either. It's what Sigal Barsade and Olivia A. O'Neill referred to years ago as "companionate" love—love that's based on warmth, affection, and connection. The duo is well known for their studies and writing on the positive value of creating emotional cultures in business. The more love coworkers feel at work, the more engaged they are, say the pair. "People who worked in a culture where they felt free to express affection, tenderness, caring, and compassion for one another were more satisfied with their jobs, committed to the organization, and accountable for their performance."[2]

Some ways leaders can show love in the workplace include:

- caring—and not just lip service—without expectations of anything in return
- gratitude/praise/reward for a job or project well done
- authenticity in relationships with others across all levels
- compassion for others, including their families and their situations
- respect for everyone, no matter their job title or position
- making *it* fun—whatever *it* is

"WHY" MATTERS

Beyond the words spoken, understanding the reasons we do things matters. I picked up that bit of knowledge from the great book *Start with Why* by Simon Sinek. After reading it, I even gave copies to all the managers at MarineMax.

Source of Motivation

All of us, whether we're a leader, administrator, line worker, or something else, should take the time to think about why we do our jobs. What is it that motivates us to show up to work every day? It's not just about getting a paycheck. Companies and their leaders need to take the time for a similar assessment.

Achieving true excellence as a person or as a company requires an understanding of the *why* in addition to the *what* and the *how*. That type of understanding creates the benchmark, provides the knowledge, and leads to the caring that has the power to drive performance at top levels.

Usually when someone is asked what they do for a living or what their company does, they answer with a generalization—"I sell cars," "I service this product," or "The company builds semiconductors." The person answering the question then generally offers some physical details on what they do and how they do it. Few people consider the true *why*.

For example, a semiconductor company manufactures semiconductors. The factory technician monitors assembly-line robots. But on closer examination, the *why* is that the small part a semiconductor company provides connects people through electronic devices. The factory technician is really an efficiency expert who is incredibly proud of the precision of her machines and how they can transform the way we live our lives.

Greater Purpose

Why is the differentiator between doing a job and contributing to a greater goal or purpose. The latter is what matters—especially to younger generations—and what each of us needs to consider in pursuit of excellence.

At MarineMax, we devoted a lot of time and effort to figuring out *why* the company and our people do what we do. Sure, we sell and service boats—that's the *what*. We talk about how we do what we do, too, like via our mobile service trucks. But that's not why each of us gets up every day or what motivates us to do our very best for our customers, our company, and ourselves.

Our *why* is *we change people's lives*. We do that by connecting them with the enjoyment, excitement, and fulfillment of being on the water, spending time with family and friends. In fact, most of our teams begin every workday reflecting on that *why* as a positive force to promote excellence—it's what drives us.

Think about it. We don't just sell or service a product; we change people's lives through the experiences of boating. That's a calling and an inspiration, and is important whether yours is a company that sells cell phones, video games, or widgets.

If you think the *why* behind a public company like MarineMax is a bit implausible, think about boating in general. Whether someone opts for a small dinghy on a pond, a comfortable powerboat on a lake, or an oceangoing yacht, it is often a family activity or one spent with friends. People buy boats as a recreational choice to bring people, friends, and families together so they can make lasting memories over a lifetime. Regularly, wherever I go, parents—their kids too—thank me for helping them discover this pastime they can all enjoy together.

That's MarineMax and its people's purpose, the foundation of our culture, and what powers our actions every day. We know we are making an impact in a positive way.

Crucial Aspect of Caring

What's your *why*? As workforces and workspaces change, the purpose behind what individuals and organizations do is especially important—and not just as a motivator. You and your company must work hard to prove you care. If you don't, stakeholders won't bother with you, regardless of the quality of your product or service or the remuneration you provide.

This is especially true with younger generations—they won't stay with a company if they're unhappy, and they're not afraid to jump ship in a heartbeat. According to a recent Randstad Workmonitor study of 35,000 workers, 70 percent of all workers today are open to changing jobs. In fact, nearly a third of Gen Z and millennial workers are actively on the lookout to change jobs.[3]

If those numbers aren't convincing enough, consider that more than half of all Gen Z and millennials prioritize their happiness, and would quit a job if it prevented them from enjoying life. Younger generations want their employer's values to align with their own. Nearly half of both millennials (48 percent) and Gen Z (49 percent) say they wouldn't accept a job that didn't align with their values on social and environmental issues.[4]

Now it's your turn to think about what drives you to show up for work each day. What fuels your purpose?

These are questions every organization and individual needs to consider. After all, without purpose or direction, how can you or your company know where you're going, measure performance levels, or do your very best?

CULTIVATING YOUR TEAMS

In the face of all kinds of challenges, relentless caring, both internally and externally, is essential. After all, happy teams equate to happy customers, and happy customers lead to more customers and better bottom lines.

ASSESS YOUR LEADERSHIP: FIND YOUR *WHY*

Let's start with the basics to create a solid foundation to build and improve upon. Here are some questions to consider as you search for your purpose and the purpose of your organization. Consider each of these questions first from a personal standpoint and then again as an organization.

- **What specifically do you do?**
- **How do you do it?** For example, if you're in sales, you likely meet, greet, and listen to the needs and wants of customers. Often that's how you can create the type of excitement that leads to performance excellence. The answers to what and how you do what you do primarily appeal to your logic or right side of the brain. Your real why involves your emotions, which is the left side of the brain.
- **Why do you do what you do?** The answer to that question may be difficult to put into words. For example, why do you love your spouse or your children or a significant other?
- **What gets you up every day, other than a job or to make money?** That can be your why.
- **What is the desired outcome or goal of what you do?**

Here are four ways to demonstrate relentless caring in your organization.

1. Stop talking and start listening.

A crucial part of relentless caring is listening to your team members. Even making time for a team member to talk about themselves or their families lets them know you care. Once again, this may seem insignificant, but it can make a big difference.

Listen attentively to help that person resolve a problem and don't interrupt. Help someone make an idea their own too. These are important ways to cultivate relationships with your teams.

When you genuinely make a personal connection, you'll be rewarded with positive results. By listening, you are communicating that you respect that person, and who doesn't want to be respected and appreciated?

2. Meet regularly, but don't waste time.

Strong connections can be fostered by regular, frequent, and well-run meetings. Those get-togethers—virtual and otherwise—are a symbol of caring if you respect everyone's time and make the meetings dialogues instead of monologues. Meetings shouldn't simply be a rehash of what was said last week or only about planning or laying out strategy. They should also be a time to celebrate successes and opportunities as well as a venue to hand out praise at the team and individual levels and talk about ways to do better.

At MarineMax, dealerships hold daily informal stand-up meetings. These are a great place to connect, share insights, recognize accomplishments, debrief about challenges, and reiterate messages that are essential to building and maintaining a strong culture.

Plenty of people complain about too many meetings, whether online or in person. But in my experience the problem isn't the meeting—it's the meeting's organizer.

Meetings are an essential interaction; without them, the message sent is, "We don't care," especially with so many people now working remotely. So, instead of simply cutting back on meetings or enduring the endless complaints about them, reassess your meeting agendas. Imagine meetings that team members actually want to attend! It's possible with the right approach. We'll talk more about this later.

3. Give gifts (including the gift of positive feedback).

Gift giving done right is a way to let your team know you care. The right kinds of gifts are crucial. The most impactful ones are not always what you would think of, and they don't have to cost lots of money. (Remember the country ham discount from earlier in the chapter.)

Regular and consistent recognition of a job well done is one of the most powerful gifts you can give and should be standard procedure. Monetary and compensatory rewards shouldn't be reserved for only executives or the sales teams either.

Pictured are team members on an awards trip to the British Virgin Islands on our Aquila Power Catamarans.

MarineMax adds a motivational boost for its teams by sharing the criteria/qualification for any potential awards with team members' families and significant others. It's a surprisingly powerful tool for greater achievement when those we care about know and understand the *why* behind extended work hours or the extra time spent with a client.

For example, at one team and family/partners get-together, we announced an upcoming free family trip to the Bahamas for the annual top sellers, managers, or regional presidents. No family; no problem. Take special friends instead. To make the goal even more enticing, we made the announcement following a video about a previous trip we'd sponsored to the Bahamas.

We do motivational achievement awards with our other team members, too, from top financial and insurance team members to marina staff, yacht brokers, technicians, and boat detailers. Awards range from gift cards or cash to free dinners and beach days for families and more. Basically, we offer rewards to all stakeholders involved with delivering the right experience for our customers.

In December our dealerships hold holiday parties, and a team member dresses as Santa Claus to hand out age-appropriate presents to all the children of team members. No kids? Again, no problem. Everyone also receives a cash holiday bonus.

This is relentless caring. We go out of our way to recognize our team members' families and significant others. On awards trips and at team gatherings, and in interactions, we always thank the spouses / significant others and families for their contributions to the success of our team members and the company. That may be something else that sounds trivial, but the reality is it reinforces a culture that values team members and their families as part of our family.

4. Provide outstanding healthcare benefits (yes, it's possible and affordable).

Quality healthcare at an affordable price is one of the greatest gifts you can give your team, and one that's especially appreciated because it can make a huge difference in someone's life. There's no question that finding or putting together a top policy can be a challenge. However, it is possible and can be within reach even for small companies. You need to be willing to try something new and partner with companies that can make it a reality.

Too often organizations think they are saving money by offering employees an insurance plan with higher employee out-of-pocket costs and minimal benefits when the reality is the opposite. Poor healthcare benefits can lead to a lack of loyalty and commitment, added financial stress on workers, poor mental health, and disengagement—or, even worse, departure from the company. All of that can negatively affect an organization's bottom line.

MarineMax wanted to provide our teams the best plan possible, so we made the decision to self-insure and partner with what we believed was the right administrator, a Dallas-based firm then called GPA, now Imagine360 (www.imagine360.com). It was a game changer. The result has been world-class, award-winning healthcare for our teams. Some of the benefits include cost savings for our company, no balance billing for team members, no premium increases in the past eight years, reduced deductibles, less expensive prescriptions, 24/7 access, and so much more. (If you're interested in more specifics about our model, check out the addendum at the end of this book on how your organization can develop its own world-class healthcare model.)

TAKEAWAYS

- Relentless caring is good for you, your organization, and your customers.
- Relentless caring isn't difficult, but it takes focus and commitment up front from the organization and its leadership.
- When people know you care, they in turn care about you *and* your business.
- Success in transforming a culture is about laying out a goal, then repeatedly reinforcing the goal through actions to create new habits, which eventually lead to changing a culture. (Goal→Repetition→Habit→Culture)
- Meetings done right matter and demonstrate to your teams that you care.
- Choose your words carefully with your teams as well as your customers. That's because word choice reveals attitude.
- Words should be motivational and convey personalized respect and recognition.
- *Love* is a popular workplace buzzword. Managers and leaders are supposed to give their teams more love so they are more engaged and committed. This goes beyond simple respect to encompass genuine caring for team members as individuals.
- A crucial part of relentless caring is listening to your team members. Even making time for a team member to talk about themselves or their families lets them know you care.

- An important way to cultivate relationships with your team includes helping someone make an idea their own.
- Gift giving is an effective way to demonstrate relentless caring and doesn't have to cost a lot of money. Positive reinforcement and acknowledgment of a job well done is a great no-cost gift and should be standard across all levels of your company.
- Quality healthcare at an affordable price is one of the greatest gifts you can give your team. It can be accessible and affordable even for small companies.

Chapter Two

Kindness Comes First, Profits Follow

Profit is not a dirty word.

—A LESSON LEARNED EARLY IN BUSINESS

Customers don't forget—ever!

Today's soaring gasoline prices and long lines at the gas pump are nothing new. During the OPEC Oil Embargo in the mid-1970s, service station allotments of gasoline were tightly rationed, but fuel for marine use was not. By this time, I had turned entrepreneur and partnered with my uncle in Sarasota, Florida, to open and operate Gulfwind Marine, a small boat dealership in nearby St. Petersburg.

Gulfwind Marine in the early years.

Because our gasoline for marine use was not restricted like that for automobiles, I figured this was a great opportunity to share what we had with our customers to use in something other than boats—their car or truck, for example. It was our way of letting our customers know we cared and considered them like family. We didn't expect anything in return. Yet that kindness has been paid back many times across the years in the form of repeat business and referral customers.

In fact, not long ago I was at a boat show in St. Petersburg when a couple approached me, profusely thanking me for sharing gasoline supplies with them when they bought their first boat nearly a half-century ago. Over the years, the couple has returned to purchase seven additional boats from us. Such is the power of relentless caring.

THE CURSE OF SHORT-TERM VISION

Caring reconciles with profits, period. Short-term pursuit of profits is myopic when considering the long-term benefits of a more-than-satisfied customer willing to do business with you again and again and tell their friends about you too.

After all, it costs five times more to attract a new customer than retain an old one, according to research from ITA Group, experts in driving engagement and bottom-line results.[1] That may not translate into spending that much more money at a smaller company, but it still means an extra cash expense that can cramp already tight bottom lines has been prevented. And it's an unnecessary expense if a company and its leaders take the time to truly care about their customers and their teams. That's a big part of why relentless caring is a differentiator that benefits all participants and creates an empowered culture in which delivering beyond expectations is second nature.

At a large company like MarineMax, much of the cost of acquiring a new customer is the expense of marketing through boat shows. That literally amounts to hundreds of thousands of dollars per show, factoring in the cost of moving the equipment, travel, and accommodations for our team participants. Plus, that's money spent with no assurance of gaining a customer. So, it makes lots more financial sense to invest in keeping happy customers through services that exceed their expectations.

EMPOWERED CULTURE

Think of relentless caring as customer service on steroids that happens naturally when you instill in your teams a specific culture to exceed customer expectations and empower those team members to do what it takes to live the culture no matter the financial cost.

Consider that a customer buys your service or product with certain expectations of outcome or performance, only to be delighted or disappointed. The cost of the product may vary, but the delight or disappointment is the same. The excitement of a low price or "hot deal" is soon forgotten as a result of a bad experience. That's worth repeating: the excitement of a low price is soon forgotten in the face of a bad experience. How a leader and their team does or does not handle that disappointment lays the groundwork for future sales and profits; it's that simple. It could be in the form of repeat business—or lack thereof—or positive or negative referrals.

WORTH THE PRICE

MarineMax is a one-price retailer—we price our products at a discount off the manufacturer's suggested retail price and don't negotiate that price. The price includes the services of a captain to teach customers and their families/friends how to use the boat; extended service warranties; mobile service teams that, usually at no extra charge, come to the boat, wherever it is, to take care of repairs or problems; and various other periodic gifts as part of the MarineMax family.

Avoiding Contradictions

Early on at MarineMax, just before the IPO, I kept asking myself and talking with our team about how contradictory it was to ask customers to be a part of our *family* and then to figuratively put on the boxing gloves and duke it out over price negotiations. After all, you don't negotiate with your family. I was leaning toward MarineMax offering fair one-price selling.

There was plenty of pushback from sales team members and managers who argued that customers wanted to negotiate price. Some team members threatened to leave the company since they believed that one-price selling would destroy the business. So, we hired a company to hold customer focus groups to look at, among other things, whether customers want to negotiate when buying a boat or yacht. Those groups answered, "Yes"—customers did want to negotiate price.

We then followed up with another question: "Why do you want to negotiate price?" And the groups answered, "To get the best and lowest price." The next question then posed to the focus groups was, "If the price presented was a discounted price from MSRP (manufacturer's suggested retail price) and not negotiable, would you still want to negotiate?" All the focus groups answered the same way: "We would not negotiate because we hate the confrontational process and would always question whether we could have gotten an even lower price."

Wow! Those focus groups validated that the right thing to do for customers is not to put them through the negotiation process, which itself is dishonest in most cases and certainly not practicing relentless caring toward our sales team or our customers.

When we implemented the one-price approach, MarineMax ended up losing several sales team members whose sales tactics were based solely on price. They simply couldn't adjust to this new customer-friendly pricing approach. Ultimately, though, the team members that accepted this (then-new) one-price approach found that they and the customers appreciated the honest pricing and hassle-free buying experience.

Beyond the Price

That said, even though MarineMax offers good prices and services well beyond those of our competition, sometimes potential customers will opt to buy the same product elsewhere at a bigger discount. When equipment problems arise, though, those same people turn to us for assistance.

Somehow that $10,000 perceived savings is forgotten when it's the Fourth of July, six friends are sitting on your boat waiting to head out, the boat stops suddenly, and the seller is nowhere to be found. And even if you could reach them, they certainly won't come out to take care of the problem.

We actually have had people in similar situations plead with us to help them, offering to pay the difference in the boat's original cost (had they purchased it from us) if only we will allow them to join the MarineMax family and receive the perks associated with that.

Or—this also happens relatively frequently—a boat manufacturer overlooks installing certain required equipment on your new "cut-rate cost" boat, and suddenly the Coast Guard pulls you over with a warning or even a ticket. Then, to make matters worse, you can't get the manufacturer/dealership who sold you the discounted boat to fix the problem. Those cost savings quickly evaporate as you scramble to figure out how to fix the problem yourself.

PROBLEMS ARE OPPORTUNITIES

There's no exact across-the-board formula on how to exceed customer service expectations; every situation is different. Instead, it's about attitude, approach, and execution across all levels with caring top of mind regardless of the necessary effort or expense involved. That's a wide-open statement. But with the right people in the right jobs, and sincerity, trust, transparency, and honesty at the forefront, it works, is a replicable approach, and succeeds again and again. (More on the details later.)

Exceeding customer expectations is also about having a relentless and repetitive focus on an organization's positive values and developing a culture that treats customers as we would want to be treated. That means continual and honest communication with your teams on what works and what doesn't. In the case of MarineMax, that communication includes daily sharing and discussion of NPS responses to help ingrain the importance of and focus on customer service and caring.

A MarineMax dealership in Minnesota sold a boat to a customer who was excited to take his family and friends out on Lake Minnetonka (near Minneapolis) to watch the Minnesota Vikings football game on the boat's big-screen TV. Unfortunately, when the buyer took his friends out on the boat and tried to turn on the TV, it no longer worked.

The customer was upset, but he didn't call the dealership. Instead, when the dealership followed up with its NPS questionnaire, the customer gave the company a poor score. (NPS, or Net Promoter Score, is the metric MarineMax uses to measure customer satisfaction.) Had the interaction stopped there, the disgruntled customer might never have purchased another boat from MarineMax. Worse, he likely would have urged his friends to avoid MarineMax.

But, when the MarineMax store manager saw the low NPS, he personally reached out to the disgruntled customer first. Learning about the broken television, he immediately took responsibility for the problem, no questions asked, brought a new television out to the boat on the lake, and installed it. Additionally, the store manager bought the customer two tickets to the next Vikings home game and delivered those tickets to the customer's home as an additional apology for the inconvenience.

You may think that's over the top. But that's delivering beyond expectations; that's creating the WOW factor. The same customer has since bought multiple boats from our company, more than making up for the extra expense of the new television, its on-site installation, and the football tickets. Relentless caring earned the company a customer for life simply by turning a problem into an opportunity through empathy and caring.

Granted, that Minnesota boat and its associated faux pas was a big expense. But the faulty product could just as easily have been a $35 hair dryer that didn't work, a $1,000 cell phone with an irritating glitch, or a $150 meal that made you sick. It doesn't matter the cost of the product or service; it's how a company's leadership responds that makes the difference. It doesn't matter the amount of money someone spends; the customer needs to know you care.

In another example, one of our affiliates led a boat excursion to the Bahamas for a group of boat owners and their families. Once in the islands, one of the families ventured out on their own, away from the guided flotilla. The crystal-clear water in the Bahamas makes differentiating water depths difficult, and as a result their boat ran aground and sustained serious damages that made it inoperable. The damages were covered by the family's insurance policy, yet without a boat, their holiday would have been ruined.

But this is the MarineMax family. Another family in the flotilla welcomed the grounded travelers on their boat. Then—here's where relentless caring kicks in—to help reduce the hassles for our customer, MarineMax not only managed the boat's repairs but provided someone who brought the boat back to Florida at no charge to the family.

The goodwill gesture cost MarineMax time and money, but this was an investment in the future. The situation wasn't about casting blame; it was about turning a bad situation into an opportunity and exceeding the expectations of the customer, no questions asked. We continually remind our teams (there's that repetition again) that if a customer has a problem or encounters a problem, no matter who is at fault, it's our problem to handle and to solve.

With the Bahamas trip, the extra expense to the company was quickly recouped in the form of repeat business and repeat referrals to other customers not only from the family we helped but from the other fifty boats and their passengers on the trip as well. After all, the biggest catalyst to acquiring new customers is referrals, which come from happy customers who relay their experiences to friends and family and share the benefits of purchasing *your* product, whether it's a boat or a basketball, and the service that comes with it.

THE *WOW* FACTOR

Plenty of organizations of all sizes tout exceeding customers' expectations as something they do, but most fall short on execution. That often is because simply doing one more thing or "going the extra mile" isn't enough. To genuinely relentlessly care in a way that brings people back demands the WOW factor—delivering customer service that is so unexpectedly beyond the accepted standard that it WOWs people.

Beyond the Expected

Let's say you decide to go to dinner at an expensive restaurant. A delicious meal and great service is the expectation. When that happens, it's not really exceeding the initial expectations.

The WOW factor comes when the restaurant host greets you by name, personally helps seat you, and the waiter remembers your drink preference and tastes based on your last visit. Then the chef checks that you are enjoying the meal, and the manager drops by the table to thank you for your confidence in their services and offerings. An extra WOW is the doggie bag with your partially eaten dessert replaced by a fresh one.

All that is about ROI, or investing a portion of profits in developing repeat customers. And it works. It's a near-guarantee the diner will return, ask for the same waiter, and share their positive experiences with others.

For the last fifty years one of my favorite restaurants has been Bern's Steak House in Tampa, Florida. It's a true dining experience that consistently exceeds customers' expectations and is validated by many national awards for their food and wines. Their focus on caring for their team and customers has yielded a dining experience like no other.

Over the years I've entertained many of our team members, suppliers, and customers at Bern's. It's a great way for them to experience customer service well beyond expectations in terms of dining as we focus on delivering well beyond customer service when it comes to the boating experience. Bern's repeat business is legendary as guests return again and again and also share the experience with their family, friends, and business associates.

Anyone Can Do It

Any organization, large or small, can show that kind of caring for their customers and their teams without big financial investments. Even tiny mom-and-pop shops can (and some already do) provide that WOW in customer service—whether it's the corner dry cleaner that calls to remind a customer they are closing soon if they need their clothes that day; the neighborhood bagel shop that makes sure to bake enough of your favorite bagels for Saturday morning pickup even though you forgot to turn in your regular order; or the mega retailer that proactively follows up on a sale and quickly responds to any issues. Such is the power of relentless caring.

Delivering well beyond customer expectations isn't only for larger companies either. One marine sales and service dealership and marina in a tiny Northern Virginia town has about forty-five employees, including the owner. Every weekend the owner walks his docks, helping customers with any issues to ensure they enjoy a hassle-free boating experience. He's made a conscious effort to know the people and their families, too, because he lives relentless caring and understands how boating changes people's lives.

The owner of another small boat–component manufacturer attends as many boat shows and events as possible around the country. He doesn't do it to sell his product; he's there to share advice and wisdom with customers as well as vendors exhibiting their products.

Both are small companies with leaders who understand the WOW that comes with relentless caring.

Long-Term Goals

On a larger scale, and as I mentioned earlier, MarineMax provides free mobile repair service for its customers. That's a big deal in the marine business. Let's say someone has a boat in need of repairs on Lake Allatoona in northwest Georgia. That's about thirty miles from Atlanta. Most boat dealerships and marinas offer two repair options: the customer can bring the boat into the shop or marina for repair, or the company will charge a hefty fee to come to the boat.

MarineMax instead goes to the customer's boat, wherever it is, at little or no extra charge. And, while out on the repair call, if the team notices something else that needs fixing, they fix it free of charge. No one has to wait for authorization from the dealership either, because the company empowers our teams to take care of the extra work at no charge. After the repairs are done, the service team will inform the customer of what they did.

For example, a repair team on a service call might notice several missing snaps on a boat's canvas cover and replace them as the company's "gift" to the customer. That's WOW. That's the right thing to do, and that's something people don't forget.

Again, I learned the power of that kind of relentless caring in my days with NASA. Back then, whenever I could, I would offer to help others with whatever they were doing. It could be as simple as holding something for a technician to make their job easier or as complex as brainstorming with them to solve a vexing problem. This wasn't part of my job description, but I always offered to help others, and they never forgot that. When I needed help, they were there in an instant.

In the Corporate World

Do you still think that extra caring equaling profits is a far-fetched idea? Again, consider MarineMax. After more than twenty-five years as a public company accountable to tough shareholders and bottom lines, profits are as solid as our mantra of caring first and foremost. That's through good and bad economic times, a pandemic, and political upheaval.

It's not always smooth sailing—pun intended—but we operate with the long-term view in mind, not short-term fast profits. If a public company constantly accountable to the bottom line and its shareholders can do this so successfully, there's little excuse why a smaller and/or private business can't do it too.

DEALING WITH THE INEVITABLE NAYSAYERS

No matter the size of the business, though, there always are those who doubt the value of relentless caring. These are people who, at least initially, have difficulty reconciling bottom lines with the investment of time, people, and sometimes extra money required to take the initiative and provide over-the-top customer service, which many of them think is unnecessary. There's often pushback, too, against relentless caring for team members and their families.

That's especially true with institutional investors. They worry about norms and expectations and dollars and cents this year and next, not the nuances of caring about others first, often at the expense of immediate cash returns. For these investors, it's about quarterly financial performance with earnings and acquisitional growth top of mind, many times to the detriment of what is best for a company in the long term. Chatter or threats aside, the best leaders never lose sight of the long-term view.

At MarineMax the focus always has been to do what's best for the long term even if a decision means missing a revenue or earnings target. During the 2008–2009 economic downturn, the company maintained its long-term approach to doing business despite serious pushback from Wall Street.

At the beginning of 2008, business was great; we were moving boats and couldn't keep enough in stock. Then the market collapsed, and business went with it. Dealers had too much inventory; some wanted to cut corners on service and dump product at cut-rate prices. Our message, though, was stay the course; focus on the customer and don't drastically discount despite what's happening across the industry. We told our teams the company would take care of them; that's the MarineMax culture—we care for our customers and our team members and their families 24/7.

We had some managers that didn't get it, wanted to take shortcuts, and refused to care for their customers or teams. Our response was simple: we let go of those managers or closed their stores. Meanwhile, we worked our way through reducing inventory and stretched the company financially to take care of our people. We didn't back off our mobile customer servicing, team training, Getaways! events, or even bonuses.

To further incentivize our teams to not forget the relentless caring part of our culture and to work hard to bring MarineMax back to profitability, we instituted a bonus plan for regional presidents, store managers, business managers, and service managers. The temporary plan was based on our company sharing earnings improvements with our team leaders.

If, for example, a store experienced a $1 million loss in 2008 as a result of the economy, and cut that loss to $500,000 in 2009, the manager received a $50,000 bonus. The bonus plan also exemplified the MarineMax culture of thinking long-term as well as caring for our teams and their families in tough times. Today many of those managers are still with our company and remember and appreciate being taken care of in the tough times.

During that time, some of our investors had urged us to further chop expenses and return to higher profitability, but we stuck to our long-term approach. MarineMax's stock price plummeted. I told our teams and investors at the time that if the stock goes down, it doesn't hurt you if you don't sell; don't fret what happens with the stock price on a daily basis; ours is a long-term approach.

We did not chase Wall Street's approval back then, and we still don't. From a high of $36.58/share as of April 2006, during the recession, the price of MarineMax stock dropped to $2.03 a share on January 23, 2009. But we held on to our long-term optimism, and it paid off. After the recession, we ended up with a strong balance sheet and stronger teams more dedicated than ever to the company and its leadership, and MarineMax survived and prospered.

How prosperous was MarineMax? By May 2021, MarineMax stock was trading in the $65 range. There have been other bumps. As of mid-2022, the stock was trading in the $40-plus range.[2] But the point is that the long-term approach to doing business works.

Challenges are opportunities. The lessons learned from that recession have carried us through ups and downs since then. After the 2008–09 downturn, we brainstormed with our teams on how we could learn from our mistakes and become better. We changed how we stock unsold inventory. The lesson we had learned was that excess inventory makes sales easier but becomes a burden when business slows and the product ages. More than a dozen years later, we still repeat the lesson regularly today so our teams don't forget.

Most importantly, after the recession our leaders more than ever understood the power of relentless caring and the importance of not losing sight of a company's long-range goals in favor of quick-hit gains. Our long-term view prevailed those years ago, and it still does with the help of tireless explanation and repeatedly sharing positive outcomes. Both tactics are powerful catalysts to help convert the doubters. In other words, it is important to continually demonstrate to naysayers why and how relentless caring toward your customers and teams grows a business and profits.

RIGHT HIRING

Important, too, as mentioned earlier, is that the right hiring decisions matter to the long-term success of any business. We recognized that early at MarineMax.

I'm always reading, listening, and learning from others how we can become better at what we do. That's how I learned about Topgrading, a process developed by Bradford D. Smart, PhD, an industrial psychologist and author of a number of bestsellers, including *Topgrading: The Proven Hiring and Promoting Method That Turbocharges Company Performance* and *Foolproof Hiring.* Topgrading is a twelve-step process to help identify the "A" players for your team (more details on Topgrading in the next chapter). With some of our senior management assisting, I approached our board about making a sizable investment to explore bringing Topgrading into our hiring and promotion process.

We wanted to engage Brad to look at how Topgrading could help us. Several of our board members and team members thought the investment of thousands of dollars to bring in Brad was too much, offered questionable returns, and would disrupt short-term profits. So, I met with the board and detailed how caring for our teams meant making sure each person was in the right job, which would contribute to them being happy and successful in their careers. Topgrading, I explained, could help us do that, as well as make sure we had a team of grade A players and provide the tools for others to improve.

I also provided each of the board members and our senior team with a copy of Brad's book to help them learn more about Topgrading's potential benefits. Then at every opportunity I talked about how the Topgrading process, with its comprehensive look at a person's professional expertise and personality traits, could help us improve our hiring and further cement our culture of relentless caring. Of course, Topgrading alone isn't enough to guarantee correct hiring and promotion every time. (I'll talk more about our hiring practices in the second part of this book.) But it does help provide valuable insights.

Continually reinforcing the message that Topgrading worked helped persuade the naysayers to allow us to hire Brad. It worked. We invested in help from his team and eventually incorporated Topgrading into our processes.

The positive reinforcement didn't stop after the board and our senior team bought into Topgrading either. We worked hard back then to show the board the subsequent successes of what at the time was a new and different approach. We introduced our new team members to the board and showed them how the Topgrading approach had improved our hiring and promotion numbers. Instead of hiring A players three out of twelve times, which, according to Brad, is the industry success rate without Topgrading, MarineMax's success rate climbed to more than nine out of ten. Promotion successes experienced a similar uptick with the use of the Topgrading approach. The bottom line was that formally incorporating Topgrading into our people processes helped make the difference financially and beyond.

Almost twenty-five years and tens of thousands of hires and promotions later, we continue to justify the expense of and rely on our Topgrading-based method. Remember, to ingrain a process, procedure, or attitude into a company's culture requires repetition, repetition, repetition. That's not being irritatingly repetitious; that's developing a habit that eventually becomes part of a culture.

Too many people and their organizations get what they want and then move on to the next goal without continually reinforcing the positive effects of the previous goal or win.

Commitment

From the beginning of the COVID-19 lockdown, we told our teams we would take care of them—salaries as well as supplemental income if store performance dropped due to the economic slowdown. We wanted our people to concentrate on their health and their families' health. These people are our family, and that's our culture.

Early on some team members pushed back, worried about the short-term hit to our bottom line and what would happen. But as is the MarineMax way, we took the long-term view. As the weeks of lockdown stretched into months, worries of short-term losses were forgotten as customers focused on family and getting out on the water, and our business boomed.

Even if the boating boom hadn't happened—and it doesn't always—we still would have maintained the long-term view. That's simply what makes good business sense.

FORGET THE REASONS WHY NOT

The typical excuses companies and their leaders give for fast profits at the expense of caring range from "We can't afford it" to "Why bother?" and "We don't have the staff or time." Those excuses make little sense in today's highly competitive customer-driven markets.

A company can't afford not to take care of a customer so that they keep coming back and tell their friends about their positive experiences. As far as staffing issues go, companies today also can't afford staff that contribute to a continual loss of customers.

One bad hire costs not only the money spent on that person and on hiring their replacement, but also the price of lost current and prospective customers. A company can't even accurately know how many people that person has sent away and down the street to buy the same product from someone else. (More on that in the next chapter.)

IT'S YOUR TURN

As you can see, relentless caring *is* a proven profitable approach to business. However, it also is a different, outside-of-the-norm way of thinking that at times requires steadfast courage to implement and maintain.

This isn't about token talk or actions; it's about genuine concern for others, creating friendships and relationships, and putting others first 24/7. When that happens with any business, profits will follow.

Now it's your turn to transform yourself and your company, to understand how to manage from the heart, to identify and live your values in all that you do, to learn what it takes to make the right hiring and promotion decisions, to hone your communications skills, to be accountable to your teams and your customers, to be willing to take risks, and to relentlessly care. With these tenets of business success in play, you and your company will come away the big winners.

We will delve deeper into these tenets in the following pages. So, get ready to not just do business, but to create long-term business relationships, friendships, and extended families that can help any business thrive in good economic times and bad.

SIX TENETS TO SUCCESS

1. Get the people equation right.
2. Stop talking and start active listening.
3. Live your values 24/7.
4. Be accountable to your teams and your customers.
5. Be relentlessly persistent.
6. Be willing to take calculated risks; without them there's no reward.

WHERE TO START

Let's begin the journey with an assessment of your starting point, where you and your company are now on the relentless caring spectrum. When you know that, it's easier to set goals and implement solutions to achieve those goals.

ASSESS YOUR LEADERSHIP: DO YOU CARE?

Where do you stand on the relentless caring spectrum? Let's begin the journey with an assessment of your starting point, where you and your company are today. When you know that, it's easier to set goals and implement solutions to achieve those goals.

Here are a few questions to ask of yourself and again of your organization. Rate your responses to each question on a scale of 0 to 20 points or as indicated.

1. **Do I sincerely ask team members how they are doing and remember previous interactions?** If yes, you earn 20 points.
2. **Do I ask team members about their families and remember previous interactions?** If yes, you earn 15 points.
3. **When interacting with team members and customers, do I let them speak more than me?** If the answer is yes for team members, you earn 15 points; a yes for customers earns you 10 points.
4. **Have I gone out of my way to congratulate team members on successes?** If the answer is yes, you earn 10 points.
5. **Do I live the values that I profess?** Yes gets you 20 points.
6. **Have I surrounded myself with A players?** Yes earns 10 points.

7. **Have I done a good job in letting team members and customers know that I care about them and their families?** Yes equals 20 points.

Now total your score:

- **A score of 100 to 110:** Great job; you're a caring leader.
- **50 to 99:** You're on your way but need to improve.
- **Less than 50:** There's lots of work to be done.

TAKEAWAYS

- Relentless caring isn't about buzzwords and false promises; it's living caring 24/7 in all you do.
- A short-term pursuit of profits is myopic when considering the long-term benefits of a more-than-satisfied customer willing to do business with you again and again and tell their friends too.
- Think of relentless caring as customer service on steroids.
- Exceeding customer expectation requires relentless focus on an organization's positive values and developing a culture that treats customers as you would want to be treated.
- Lots of organizations tout great customer service, but most fall short because simply doing one more thing or "going the extra mile" isn't enough. To genuinely

relentlessly care in a way that brings people back again and again requires the WOW factor—delivering customer service that is so unexpectedly beyond the accepted standard that people notice.

- Continuous reinforcement of a message helps convert naysayers and establishes the importance of the message.
- Too often people and their organizations get what they want and then move on to the next goal without continually reinforcing the positive effects of the previous goal or win. To ingrain a process, procedure, or attitude into a company's culture requires repetition, repetition, repetition.
- Hiring right is essential to the long-term success of any organization.
- Topgrading—with hiring and promotion—is a proven approach to help ensure yours is a team of A players.
- The pursuit of short-term profits can be shortsighted in good economic times and bad.
- No matter the chatter, the threats, or the external and internal pushback, the best leaders never lose sight of the long-term view.
- The typical excuses organizations and their leaders give for fast profits at the expense of caring range from "We can't afford it" to "Why bother?" and "We don't have the staff." Those excuses make little sense in today's highly competitive customer-driven market. An organization can't afford not to care.

Part II

THE SIX TENETS OF RELENTLESS CARING

Chapter Three

Tenet 1: Get the People Equation Right

It's not just a job; we are all family.

—A LESSON LEARNED EARLY IN BUSINESS

Always surround yourself with high-performing people—the "A" players who fit your culture. That's not an earth-shattering revelation, but it is an essential tenet of success that surprisingly few companies master. Almost three of every four hires are *not* the A player you need, according to a recent CareerBuilder survey.[1]

When you identify and populate your teams with the A players (the top 10 percent of talent, according to Brad Smart, *Topgrading* author) and let them know you care about them and their families, managing is easy. Conversely, surround yourself with C players—those individuals below the top 35 percent of talent—says Brad, and managing is tough and frustrating. After all, how can you sincerely praise and show appreciation for poor performers?[2]

Yes, there always will be C players, but managers must have the tools to help those less-than-ideal performers become A and B players or find more appropriate jobs internally or elsewhere. That sounds elitist and cold, but it's reality.

Consider the following:

- Your people make your company, so choose wisely. Too few corporate leaders live that mantra. They may talk a good talk, but in the end they usually believe that, as the leaders, they are the company. Wrong! The opposite is true.
- With competition today so intense and margins and consumer resources so tight, no matter the size of the company, you can't afford to not have as many A players as possible.
- With these limited dollars and resources, the more A players on your team, the greater the likelihood your organization can sustain success.

IDENTIFYING TOP TALENT[3]

Bradford D. Smart, PhD, author of *Topgrading*, typifies talent as A, B, and C players. Here's the breakdown:

- **A Player:** top 10 percent of talent available
- **B Player:** next 25 percent of talent
- **C Player:** below the top 35 percent of talent

Initially I had doubts about Brad's breakdown of the various levels of talent (see box). But our more than two decades of hiring, managing, and promoting team members has validated his initial assessment many times. Today our teams at MarineMax refer to people as A, B, and C players in terms of their individual talent levels and someone's promotability, potential to benefit from coaching, and which jobs would align with their competencies. The MarineMax goal is a 90 percent success rate when it comes to hiring and promoting A players along with a very low percentage of C players.

Surrounding yourself with A players begins with the leader; they must be an A player and build their team of A players. Brad's studies and our experience over the years have validated that A players will not work very long for B or C players. Put another way, A players attract other A players.

Additionally, although leaders are often hesitant to admit it, the presence of underperformers can upset A players as well as the entire operation. I remember the sales team at one store included three outstanding A players and one inherited underperforming C player. The store's manager tried extensively to coach the C player how to improve, but nothing changed.

Eventually the A player sales team members went to the manager and told him they would handle the extra prospects and customer workload until he could find an A player to join their team. Once the C player was reassigned to a new role as service adviser, the overall sales performance of the store improved. And so did the entire store's morale because not only had fellow sales team members been frustrated by the underperformer, but the business office and service department had been too. The impact of one misplaced C player reverberated across the organization. When the tenured team member was reassigned, he was happier and shined in his new role too.

SETTING YOUR TEAMS UP TO SUCCEED

All this talk about the best players doesn't mean an organization should pursue only those people who act, think, or talk the same, perform the same way, or share the same ideas. After all, your customers aren't all the same either. They don't believe the same, act the same, or make decisions the same way. Each person is unique and so is every manager and team member; each has their own strengths and weaknesses.

The best leaders recognize these human differences and enable their team members to excel at what they do best. They help them identify their strengths and weaknesses rather than force them to conform to a single predefined mold.

Over the years I've also learned that you can leverage someone's strengths, but it's very difficult to overcome their weaknesses. That's why it's so important to have someone in the right job that capitalizes on their strengths and manages their weaknesses as needed. Keep in mind, too, we—myself included—all have strengths and weaknesses.

I'm reminded of a quote famously (and falsely) attributed to Albert Einstein, "Everyone is a genius. But if you judge a fish by its ability to climb a tree, it will live its whole life believing that it is stupid."[4]

THE WRONG JOB

Managing borderline B and C players is a tough challenge for managers because, as happened with the sales team member above, coaching generally doesn't elevate someone to a high B or solid A player. Instead, it's often better to redeploy the underperformer to a position where they can perform at a higher level with the goal of improving their own self-worth and happiness. That's relentless caring for those C players.

Do It Right

To be fair and relentlessly care about your teams also takes coaching, honest reviews, and a plan for each team member that includes accountability and specific time frames for improvement. Done properly, that facilitates the C player being transferred to a new role, demoted, or even separated from your organization. It helps the C player recognize, too, that they are not in a role that benefits them or the organization. After all, a person usually is happier when they are enjoying their job and doing well.

Another reason to invest the time and effort is that proper documentation in handling an underperformer can prevent lawsuits in the event of separation and sometimes even help you avoid the expense of severance packages. Obviously, some nonperforming team members are satisfied with their low performance and are simply waiting to be fired. But at least with coaching, performance reviews, and documentation, the cost of the fire or redeployment can be minimized.

Again and again when we redeploy a C or B team member, the A team members invariably say, "Thank you," or "It's about time."

At MarineMax we continuously repeat to our managers, "Surround yourself with the right team, and let them know that you care about them and their families." It's not a broken record; it's reality. The right team members in the right jobs make a manager's job better.

We had one store manager who spent a lot of his time dealing with a business manager who was misplaced in her job. The result was not only loss of company income, but just like with the above stories, a frustrated sales team and issues with our lenders.

Once the manager brought in an A player as business manager, the team's frustration level dropped, the business office delivered greater profits, and the sales team and customers had a much better experience. The store's overall financial performance and NPS ratings improved too. And that's all the result of correcting one misplaced team member. Can you imagine the dysfunction possible if several team members are in the wrong jobs, and the potential difference replacing all of them could make for an organization? It's mind-boggling.

Caring About Your Team

A top sales producer at MarineMax—I'll call him Bob—is very different from other sales leaders. Bob's Caliper Profile—an assessment of his personality and motivation—revealed he has very little empathy for others. In other words, Bob doesn't really understand or care about the feelings of his customers or team members. Normally this might limit his ability to sell. However, Bob's gregariousness, attention to detail, and intelligence is so spot-on that customers trust and enjoy working with him and continually return to do business with him. He is a valued sales team member and in a perfect position in the company.

At one point, Bob was promoted to management. But that stint was brief—he's back in sales now—because both he and our team realized he didn't enjoy managing and it wasn't his greatest strength. All too often managers and leaders promote successful team members beyond their strengths, usually in pursuit of recognition, and with disastrous results. It's important to help your team members stretch their skills so they can grow, learn, and become better. But true caring also means following up to make sure that team member is happy and doing well with their new responsibilities. If not, as a leader you must be willing to make the necessary changes.

THE RIGHT LEADERS TOO

That lesson of having the right people in the right jobs is something else I learned in my days working on the space station simulation. When tough and quick decisions—especially around things that are life-threatening—have to be made, the right person in command makes a difference. I remember another twenty-eight-day stint in the test chamber that had to be suddenly aborted midway through when a life-support system failed, jeopardizing the lives of the four people inside the chamber. Fortunately this time our leader could handle the pressure of the moment and made the right decisions that may have prevented injuries and saved lives.

That's also when I began to realize that overall success in business and in life demands that we do a better job of identifying and designating leaders who embrace relentless caring and can actually lead. Most companies generally only get it right 50 percent of the time.[5]

I made my initial foray into entrepreneurship at age thirty, when I left the Kendall Company and opened Gulfwind Marine in the Tampa Bay area. Like most business leaders, I had to learn how to get the people equation right. It wasn't easy and took me ten years. Seriously! But I learned a lot in that decade, including:

- A degree from an elite college or university does not guarantee success; managing from the heart by relentlessly caring for your teams, customers, and the company does.
- Pay attention to the details and stay involved.
- The right assessments and testing are essential.

- With every potential new hire, it's important to conduct extensive and thorough interviews to make sure the person is a fit with the company's culture.
- In all your interactions, always recruit, recruit, recruit. You never know when you'll meet an A player.

Let's look more closely.

Pay Attention to the Details and Stay Involved

As is typical with so many entrepreneurs, in the beginning I knew little about hiring, retaining, or promoting team members. But unlike many leaders, I understood the importance of both a relentless caring approach to leadership and of combining it with hard work. Nonetheless, I struggled to build a successful team.

Those first years in business weren't easy. There was an energy crisis gripping the nation followed by various recessions, each with its own challenges. I always knew I wanted to hire A players and tried to surround myself with them. But, like most companies, my success rate was about 50 percent. Half the hires worked out and the others didn't, which was frustrating as well as costly.[6]

One thing I learned that helps promote greater team success is when a manager gets involved in the details of the team's responsibilities and offers personalized expectations. This is about knowing what's really going on by listening to what others—team members, managers, and customers—say and do, and making sure your people are empathetic, responsive, and do everything possible to solve a challenge or need.

This isn't about a manager taking over a deal, controlling the narrative, or micromanaging their team. Micromanaging usually happens either because a manager's ego prompts them to control everything or else a team member is unable to meet performance standards. Both cases can be addressed by talking about performance in daily stand-up company meetings or through coaching sessions and confidential team member surveys.

When a manager must constantly check on and provide guidance to someone who reports to them, that raises questions as to whether the poor performer has had proper training or if they are misplaced in their current role. Most often, as I mentioned earlier, a weak team member can create frustration not only for a manager but the rest of their team as well.

No matter the industry, a manager or leader should be involved enough in the details to understand what is truly happening with their team members. With a potential sale, for example, let your sales team know it's their sale—but then also that you want to be involved in the details. Then listen in and watch the interactions. We do that all the time at MarineMax, and our managers know what's really happening and, as a result, can contribute.

Too many leaders still distance themselves from their teams, fail to connect with their customers, and often don't know what really is happening day in and day out in the business. Without that awareness, a leader or an organization can be caught off guard without a clear understanding of a situation.

BETTER CHOICES

In those early years, I kept thinking about how anyone in any company can make better people choices. What can a leader do to ensure they are populating their teams with the best possible people for the job?

As I mentioned earlier, a bad hire is a very costly mistake. The U.S. Department of Labor estimates the average cost of a bad hiring decision is at least 30 percent of the individual's first-year expected earnings. If you take an employee with an annual income of $50,000, the cost to the organization can be $15,000.[7]

Others argue the cost is actually greater. The cost of a manager mis-hire is approximately fifteen times the employee's base salary and may be even greater if the mis-hire isn't identified and removed in a timely fashion, says Brad, the *Topgrading* author.[8]

SHRM, the Society for Human Resource Management, pegs the cost of a bad hire much higher: $240,000, factoring in all the costs—from recruitment advertising fees and staff time to relocation and training fees for replacement hires, the negative impact on team performance, the disruption, the lost customers, and the weakened employer brand. Litigation fees can figure into the amount too,[9] and can be especially costly—MarineMax learned that the hard way with an executive-level mis-hire.[10]

THE SECRET TO HIRING SUCCESS

After ten years in the business, though, I discovered the secret to hiring right: personality and skills testing and assessments. An organization must invest the time, effort, and money to get it right *before* the hire. That can happen with the help of the right assessments—and not just of someone's business or technology skills. What counts are assessments that help unlock an individual's personality and their strengths and weaknesses dealing with others.

Lots of Options

Today there are all kinds of tests and assessments available at all price levels, from free to thousands of dollars per assessment. They're available online, in-person, via video, and more. The biggest caveat, though, is you usually get what you pay for, and since it is your company and its reputation and success, or lack thereof, on the line, I would think twice before picking the cheapest option. Also, it's worth noting that plenty of negatives as well as positives have been written, posted, or broadcast about personality and other types of testing as well as specialized approaches to business hiring.

However, I believe the many years of positive results with personality testing at MarineMax speak to the value of these tests. Also, plenty of free information from reliable sources is available online that addresses testing options and hiring approaches as well as suggestions on how to determine the right test and approach for you and your organization's needs. Good starting points are reputable industry organizations, including SHRM (www.shrm.org) and the Society for Industrial and Organizational Psychology (www.siop.org).

A FEW COMMON PERSONALITY TESTS

- Caliper Profile (www.calipercorp.com)
- Big Five Personality Test (bigfive-test.com)
- Birkman Method (birkman.com/the-birkman-method/)
- CliftonStrengths, formerly StrengthsFinder (www.gallup.com/cliftonstrengths/en/252137/home.aspx)
- DiSC® (www.discprofile.com/what-is-disc)
- Myers-Briggs Type Indicator® (www.myersbriggs.org/my-mbti-personality-type/mbti-basics/)
- The Attentional and Interpersonal Style assessment (www.TAISassessment.com)
- The Predictive Index (www.predictiveindex.com)

Whatever testing option or options you and your organization consider, though, do your due diligence—thoroughly research the product. Some questions to consider include:

- What do users think about it?
- What do detractors say?
- How reliable is the test as a behavior predictor?
- What traits does the test measure, and how?
- How is the test scored?
- How do individual scores compare with other people's scores?
- Are the traits measured by the assessment important in your organization?

YOUR QUESTIONS ON TESTING ANSWERED

The Association of Test Publishers explains why it's so important to do testing in business settings:

- **Why test?** Tests can help find the right person for the right job, advance an employee along a career path that makes the best use of their talents, or help put together effective teams or groups that work well together.
- **What do tests measure in business?** Certain tests help judge an applicant's suitability for a particular job or level of responsibility as well as measure aptitudes and characteristics like mechanical skills, sales abilities, or trustworthiness. Tests also can help

organizations better understand training and support needs.

- **Why do companies rely on tests?** The advantages of tests over traditional interviewing and other employee and hiring procedures include that tests are even-handed; ask the same questions of everyone; are more efficient in obtaining job-related information; are carefully screened to be fair and unbiased; and allow the candidate's answers to be compared with hundreds or thousands of others' answers to the same question under the same standard conditions.
- **Should a person be hired or promoted solely on the basis of test results?** Properly used, tests are only one part of a process that should include other steps like application forms, personal interviews, supervisor ratings, and background checks. Together these can provide a more comprehensive picture of an individual.

Source: www.testpublishers.org/testing-in-businesses

The Caliper Profile

When I first recognized the value of personality profiling in hiring, there weren't nearly as many easily accessible testing options. But as an avid researcher always looking to improve our hiring success, I learned about a testing tool called the Caliper Profile. Though Caliper traces its beginnings to 1961, I heard about it as a tool professional sports teams used to evaluate whether a prospective player's talents meshed with the rest of the team.[11] I thought at the time (and still today) that it's a great idea to know ahead of time whether a team will work well together.

The owner of our integrated computer system, IDS, introduced me to Caliper. As the MarineMax guinea pig, I took the test first. When I received the results and talked about them with a Caliper employee, I was blown away by how the test could understand my personality so well. I shared the report with my wife at the time, too, and she confirmed that the results were absolutely accurate.

Over the years I had experimented with other tests, but none had Caliper's precision. That was more than thirty years ago, and MarineMax still uses Caliper-based profiling, though we have tweaked it a bit over the years as our team has learned more about reviewing the results.

The original Caliper Profile today is owned by Talogy, which describes it as an objective assessment throughout the talent life cycle. Once an applicant or employee takes the Caliper Profile, their results are measured against one or more validated job models. Managers can easily see how well the candidate fits into the desired job role. This information can also be used later in the development cycle to onboard the employee, provide direct feedback, offer ongoing coaching support, and even develop job skills.[12]

By the time I discovered Caliper, my uncle and I had expanded our marine dealerships throughout Florida. My uncle was nearing retirement and I had taken over running the businesses. I knew our long-term success depended on better hiring practices, so we tried Caliper. It was a game changer. Finally we had an evaluation tool that accurately summarized someone's strengths and weaknesses before we ever hired them.

Hiring decisions no longer had to rely solely on (what can be) misleading personal interviews, vague comments from former employers, and often overinflated résumés. In fact, more than 60 percent of candidates lie to get a job, according to Brad, the *Topgrading* author, who is also an industrial psychologist. Those candidates get away with it, he says, because hiring companies rarely permit their managers to make or accept reference calls for fear of lawsuits. Most companies refer reference calls to their human resources departments, and they provide only basic information, like job title and employment dates. Candidates know they can hype their strengths and hide their weaker points because prospective employers will not end up talking to their managers who might cite any failures or weaknesses.[13]

At the time, we were still a relatively small company, and Caliper wasn't an inexpensive approach. But it worked, and I have always believed that you get what you pay for. Back then the cost was a few hundred dollars per test; those numbers obviously have increased over the decades since. But I still wouldn't make a people decision—and MarineMax doesn't either—whether a hire or a promotion, without reviewing someone's Caliper Profile. That's how strongly I feel about its ability to stack the deck in our company's favor. (Job candidates believed to be a good fit for MarineMax take the Caliper assessment.)

I feel as strongly about the benefits of Caliper in my personal life too. Before my wife, Irina, and I married almost twenty years ago, I gave her the Caliper Profile and shared the results of mine with her as one more way for us to better understand each other. Though that probably isn't the norm for most couples, it does further demonstrate the confidence I have in these tests. And, in this case, taking the tests and sharing our results helped us both understand each other's personalities better when communicating and understand each other's strengths, weaknesses, and differences much better when we first met and still today.

Rather than balk at spending the money for the test, organizations should think again about the cost of a mis-hire, especially over the long run. Isn't it better to get hiring right the first time? A few hundred or upwards of a few thousand dollars is a fair price to pay even for a small company to better understand a person who could represent the company. And it's not just in terms of hiring, but in better managing and coaching that person and promoting them too.

The Topgrading Approach

Even though Caliper helped our organization immediately improve our hiring success, I was determined to hone our hiring and promotion skills even further. I researched more types of testing and evaluation—and that's when I found Brad, after reading his bestseller cover to cover twice. He and his Topgrading methodology have become a catalyst for another essential piece in the intricate puzzle that is getting hiring and promotion right and people development at MarineMax. By this time we had just rolled Gulfwind Marine and four other companies into one, MarineMax, and gone public.

Brad's Topgrading is a multistep interviewing method used to evaluate candidates for hires and promotions. It's all about ensuring an organization hires A players and develops A-level teams by making the right people decisions. According to Brad's research, typically one in four hires turns out to be an A player. As I mentioned earlier, with the Topgrading approach, those numbers climb to nine of ten hires. Promotion numbers are similar.[14]

While doing my due diligence on Topgrading, I learned the process had helped General Electric and AlliedSignal among others (both success stories at the time) with hiring, developing, and promoting A players. Former General Electric CEO Jack Welch credited Topgrading with helping the company become the then most valuable company in the world.[15] I also spoke with several organizations referenced in Brad's book *Topgrading* to get their unbiased take on the effectiveness of the process.

Everyone raved about it, so I reached out to Brad to see if he would be willing to help our growing company. Rather than jump at the prospect of picking up a growing business as a client, Brad said he would be willing to help our company *if* he determined I was an A player and committed to the process. To do so, he agreed that, for a fee, he would give me a few hours of his time. I was impressed with his confidence and shocked that he wanted to be paid to talk to a potential customer. But I was also convinced Topgrading was right for our company.

Since we were a public company with an independent board of directors, I worked hard—read that as diligently and persistently—to persuade the board that the expense would be worth it. My persistence eventually paid off. When I met Brad, we immediately got along. We shared a common interest in physical fitness—including a passion for barefoot water skiing—and the commitment that if you're going to do something, no matter what it is, do it right.

Brad also quickly saw that I had done my research and was committed to successfully implementing Topgrading at MarineMax. He recognized, too, that once I committed to the process, I wouldn't give up on it. We formed a solid working relationship that we maintain today.

Over the next few years, MarineMax used the Topgrading process to help streamline its original ownership and senior management teams into A and B players and facilitate the resignations of the C players. We didn't have to fire many C players, either, because the Topgrading process and Brad helped them see they did not fit with the vision and culture of the new company. We also eventually hired a former Caliper expert to facilitate our Caliper and Topgrading efforts, though as then-CEO I took the lead on the Topgrading focus. For Topgrading to be successful, it must be led by the CEO or president and reinforced by the executive team.

More Is Better

Nearly twenty-five years and thousands of success stories later, Topgrading—along with Caliper—is in the DNA of MarineMax's hiring and promotion process. But that's not all there is. We have further honed the Topgrading twelve-step process along with Caliper and mixed it with our own approach to great success.

Today our stated hiring formula is:

- HR or a manager conducts a phone interview with a potential candidate to determine their interest and proper fit for the job and organization.
- Potential candidates are sent our proprietary online Career History Form (CHF) to complete.
- Based on the CHF response, we reject the candidate or they proceed to the next step.
- We conduct a Caliper-based profile assessment.
- Caliper experts and our HR team communicate with managers and speak with the candidate to either reject them or move them to the next step.
- We conduct a face-to-face interview with the candidate and at least two MarineMax managers/staff. The interview questions focus on what we determined from the CHF and Caliper-based profile. For example, if the candidate mentioned not being appreciated by previous bosses, we examine that in particular.
- The interviewers (usually a manager and associate or HR staff)

then rate the candidate on different attributes and subsequently write summaries and recommendations to go ahead with the candidate and the next step in the process or not.

- We contact references, which can include ex-employers as well as personal ones. With a chronological, in-depth, and structured understanding of a job candidate, it's easier to get a true picture of that individual's strengths and weaknesses when reaching out to references. For example, we could bring up something like "Mary seems to talk a lot. Was that an issue?" When a previous employer realizes you know details about an employee, you are much more likely to get an honest assessment of that candidate.
- After calls are completed, we make a final decision to proceed with a job offer or respectfully pass.

All this isn't overkill; it's about an organization getting the hiring right up front and saving what can add up to literally millions of dollars in mis-hiring expenses. Though the MarineMax process is extensive and time-consuming, an added benefit is that when someone is hired, we have a greater understanding of how to properly integrate that person into their new job and our company.

All hires are subject to this extensive process, even C-suite executives and potential new board members. We recently hired a new vice president of HR: Beth Garland. As with all other potential candidates for jobs at MarineMax, Beth started with a self-administered interview and went through all the steps. Says Beth, a twenty-year veteran HR executive, "I've never been through such an extensive, thoughtful, and thorough hiring process before. But it's all been worth the effort. I know more about myself; I have a deep understanding of MarineMax's culture, and the transition into the job has been easy and smooth as a result."

With implementation of this structured hiring process company-wide, MarineMax's success in hiring A players went from the typical 50 percent to more than 90 percent. Not many companies can claim that kind of consistent hiring success. Today, what began as a hiring and promotion rule and then a habit is now part of our culture of surrounding ourselves with the best team possible.

And, again, that's across all levels of a company. Several years ago, I approached our board about stepping back from daily operations as CEO of MarineMax. So, the board put together a search committee for my replacement that included some external candidates as well as senior managers.

Internally, several team members expressed interest in the job, including my son, Brett, who had been with MarineMax in a variety of positions since 1996. At the time, Brett was president and chief operating officer. We also looked outside the company.

After four months of meetings and interviews, the committee chose Brett to be my successor. He then spent the next two years working with me to see if he was the right fit for the company. He was, and Brett assumed the full-time president and CEO position as of October 2018.

It was a long process, but well worth the end result of finding the right person for the right job.

To Tell the Truth

Brad, in his book *Foolproof Hiring*, digs into the importance of what he says are two other essentials to hiring A players: the truth motivator and candidate-arranged reference calls with managers. The former is a part of the latter. When candidates learn that these calls are a final step in the hiring process, the low performers with inflated résumés drop out, so the company ends up basically interviewing only honest, high performers.

A players are happy to arrange reference calls with their managers, while lesser performers can't get former bosses to talk and wouldn't want that anyway, says Brad.[16]

Out of Sync or Not

Occasionally we will have a manager who questions the value of the time and effort we spend on hiring. They're usually convinced they have a better approach—with a perfect standout potential hire as proof.

I remember one manager who wanted to hire someone he insisted was the "top producing" sales agent at the competition. That kind of a superlative alone should be a red flag with a potential hire because how can anyone truly know what goes on behind someone else's closed doors? Too often perceptions become assumed realities even though they are false.

This manager didn't follow our hiring process and bypassed the Caliper-based profile and Topgrading-based interview process. Convinced this sales agent was the greatest ever, the manager hired her. It didn't take long before he realized she was a poor fit for our customer-centric company culture. He knew *some* of the boat sales that the agent lost. But how much other business did we lose discovering this person wouldn't work out in our company?

It's what you don't know about someone that is important in hiring. That's why MarineMax—as other companies should—takes the time to discover the strengths and weaknesses and successes and shortcomings of an individual and whether they are a fit for our organization's culture before they come onboard. That kind of due diligence is crucial no matter the business, industry, or job position.

Whether an organization chooses to use Caliper, Topgrading, or some other approach to human resource decision-making is an individual choice. Just remember that ordinary interviews and references don't provide nearly enough real and thorough insight into a potential hire. People stretch the truth when they're interviewed about themselves, their jobs, and their successes. Few will admit failures at previous jobs; the common answer is, "Oh, I haven't ever failed." Yeah, right!

Reference checks, too, are one of the most common ways companies learn about a potential hire, but they're relatively worthless as we've already talked about. Few past employers will offer truly honest assessments of a former coworker unless confronted, as Brad suggested earlier, with the Topgrading approach where the job candidate arranges the interviews with their manager. When that happens, the hiring process becomes more effective and infinitely more enjoyable because you know your candidates are not fooling you with a distorted profile.

NEVER STOP RECRUITING

I am constantly recruiting. That means no matter where I am or what I'm doing, I look for A players. You should always be looking for talented additions to your teams too. After all, that outstanding waiter from last night's dinner at the neighborhood bistro could just be the next top-level service adviser at your company.

MarineMax constantly reminds its teams that you never know where you'll find the next great A player. About fifteen years ago, I met Jay J. Hood. At the time he was working at an innovative manufacturer where he had developed one of the most automated boat production facilities in the industry. Eventually he retired to the British Virgin Islands, where we rekindled our friendship. At the time, Jay seemed bored with retirement, so we talked about how he might bring his skills to the MarineMax team.

Fast-forward to today. Jay's talents and experiences have helped us streamline our manufacturing at our company-owned Cruisers Yachts as well as our Polish associate, Galeon Yachts. What a gift of talent for MarineMax in the form of an associate turned friend turned business colleague. We likely never would have teamed with Jay if I hadn't always been on the lookout for A players.

THE VALUE OF A PSYCHOLOGIST

Another game changer for any organization is the addition of a psychologist on staff—or, at the very least, easy access to one for regular consultations. This isn't about simply addressing the mental health issues of your teams. (Employers must tread lightly when it comes to that given all the privacy issues involved.) It's more about learning to make the right decisions with relentless caring front and center.

Again, before you roll your eyes at the idea and expense of even a small organization hiring a psychologist, think about it. You, your teams, and your customers make decisions based on psychological characteristics, stimuli, experiences, and so much more. Motivation, training, coaching, and engagement of your teams all relate back to psychology, as do sales, marketing, and care for your customers.

The psychology of engagement or lack thereof is especially important with younger generations and remote workers. I talked in chapter one about the younger generations that won't even show up unless you care about them and make sure they know it. Executive coaching—a big chunk of it by psychologists—is a nearly $3 billion business too.[17]

Skepticism

That said, even today, not a lot of organizations or their executives and teams openly embrace the idea of regularly working with a psychologist. They may try onetime or short-term coaching for a specific purpose—leadership, team-building exercises, conflict management, or better communication—but the idea of working full-time with a psychologist elicits pushback.

As Ray Bowman points out, organizations can't afford not to at least have access to a psychologist because every business is about people, and people in business have lots of issues—from engagement to collaboration, jealousy, intrigue, communication, passive-aggressive behavior, and so on. Ray is MarineMax's senior vice president for talent and team development and a licensed psychologist.

"All of these human elements can affect one's performance. Yet so much emphasis is on accounting, processes, hiring, firing, human resources—as in payroll, IT, data processing, and HR, and now AI. People in business overlook the human being factor," says Ray.

How true. For those small companies that really can't afford a psychologist on staff, Ray offers a great solution. Why not set up an association or affiliation with a psychologist in the same way you would have a relationship with a lawyer? Remuneration could be a modest retainer or even on an hourly basis. That's a win for your organization, for your people, and your bottom line. Of course, as with anything else, don't spend your money without doing your due diligence. All psychologists are not created equal.

About five years after MarineMax embraced the Caliper and Topgrading approaches, we unexpectedly lost our on-staff Caliper expert. He had been an integral part of our hiring successes so I faced a tough job finding his replacement. But every problem is an opportunity if you can just find it. And I did. Enter clinical psychologist Ray, who was at the time in private practice in Florida. Better still, Ray liked the idea and challenge of joining our team, especially since he already had coached many of our senior executives as part of their team development.

Convinced that Ray would be a great fit with our team, especially with his coaching prowess, I set to work to convince my management team and the board of directors. It wasn't easy, especially since it would require a financial commitment as well as asking Ray to end his private practice. But, with my strong persistence and conviction, we hired him as our team's senior vice president for talent and team development.

Proof in Actions

Ray then began to meet individually with each of our senior executives. They would have private meetings or lunch followed by some initial executive coaching. (Note: sometimes starting out in a more informal setting like over lunch or coffee can help ease someone's fears or concerns about coaching, especially from a psychologist.)

In the beginning there was some pushback, as expected. But Ray demonstrated his value and gained the confidence of our leaders and the board. Some of the ways he did that were to:

- provide executive training opportunities off campus
- introduce our team to new publications for leadership training
- share articles on management and leadership for review and discussion
- act as a conflict facilitator among executives as necessary
- introduce greater structure for hiring, promotion, strategic planning, and succession planning
- refine and upgrade our Topgrading- and Caliper-based processes to improve hiring and promotion accuracy

Over the last decade, Ray has become essential to our team and its successes. He's perfected our coaching and the systems we use in hiring, promotion, and training as well as helped us build a world-class healthcare insurance plan for our teams. Additionally, Ray's duties and responsibilities expanded to include overseeing our HR department, developing a series of sales and training management videos, developing our training department, and vastly expanding our educational and development resources.

Today, after creating a team to assume all daily HR responsibilities, Ray continues as executive coach for our senior team and manages our health insurance program. This is a perfect example of how a leader can surround themselves with the best team and also accommodate an individual team member's preferences in ways that let them know you care. This is how MarineMax shows we care about Ray; his wife, Debbie; and their family.

Under Ray's guidance, too, MarineMax has revised, fine-tuned, and added to our Caliper testing and Topgrading. We have created and expanded a hiring and promotion process that's rigorous, detailed, and very structured. And it works and is embraced by our team.

Real Connection

In the process, we continue to relentlessly care about our teams and our customers, and we connect with them. Our connections aren't onetime PR stunts, the occasional summer picnic or holiday party, a Friday happy hour, or a Sunday open house. This is living our culture of relentless caring 24/7.

"Relentless caring sounds a little mushy and soft," says Ray, "but the fact is that it is a very real thing that requires conscious awareness and an ongoing appreciation for what it is. Money is great, and we all want as much of it as we can get. But people and their/our families are greater, and happiness breeds commitment and engagement and ultimately success.

"You don't have to really care about other people—but you should, and if you believe that you do not truly care sufficiently at this point, do not think that you are stuck in the muck," adds Ray. "Get some good counseling for yourself and be open to change. You will be very glad that you did. Then turn your new and improved caring and compassion into action. You will feel great—and so will those you have helped."

ASSESS YOUR LEADERSHIP: CARING ABOUT THE TEAM

A few of the ways you can relentlessly care as a leader include:

- **Disagree with respect**, not just when it comes to someone else's ideas, but with respect for that person as an individual too.
- **Act with compassion**; when people see and experience that, they know you care.
- **Listen to what others say**, learn from them, and then do the right thing.
- **Slow down and enjoy the moment**; when you see people, stop, chat, and always ask questions; people like to be seen and recognized, especially by a leader.
- **Be humble**; if you aren't, fake it until you make it.
- **Fight your ego**; support others' needs and goals with both your words and actions.

THE ISSUE OF HEALTHCARE

One of Ray's greatest contributions to MarineMax and our team is his work as helmsman for our world-renowned healthcare program. He's been honored nationally for his contributions, speaks regularly to national organizations, and even works with organizations to help them implement their own top-notch health insurance plans.

About Caring

So many organizations and leaders talk about health insurance plans, their exorbitant and always rising costs, poor coverage, exclusions, limited access, and so on. But rather than just talk about it or settle for less, MarineMax opted to put its money where its heart was—with our people—and worked to develop an innovative health insurance system that continues to provide team members with the best possible benefits.

As mentioned earlier, quality healthcare at an affordable price is a gift to your teams that's especially appreciated because it can make a huge difference in someone's life. Putting together a top health plan can be a challenge. However, quality healthcare at affordable prices isn't a pipe dream and can be within reach even for small companies. It starts with the true desire to change, the courage to stand up and try something new, and then finding the right partner companies to make it happen.

The Self-Insure Approach

In 2015 MarineMax, with its approximately 1,200 employees at the time, was spending a little over $10 million annually for its teams' medical and pharmaceutical coverage/expenses. That doesn't count the team members' share of the expenses either.

With only more cost increases on the horizon for the company and its teams, MarineMax decided enough was enough, and made the commitment to develop its own, better way. We took the risk of self-insuring and partnered with various third-party administrators, including claims managers like Dallas-based GPA (now Imagine360). The result has been world-class healthcare and insurance for our teams. Some of the benefits include: huge cost savings for MarineMax, no balance billing for team members, no premium increases for our team members over the last eight years, less expensive prescriptions, and 24/7 doctor access.

In 2021, with more than double the number of team members, MarineMax paid just $9 million for our teams' medical coverage. That's a $1 million savings from that $10 million price tag in 2015 and on coverage for a much bigger workforce. Again, that's a win-win-win for our teams, our organization, and our bottom line.

(See the Addendum at the back of the book for more about how you can replicate this successful healthcare plan without spending huge sums of money.)

Be forewarned: In the beginning, a company's shift to this new kind of health insurance is tough. Successful change takes team buy-in, and the move to a different kind of healthcare and insurance was no different. Patience and persistence from everyone was essential to ensure effective change.

Families who were used to dealing with a certain family doctor or a specialist struggled at first to find providers as part of our new network. But we worked with them to find new providers because our research had shown that without this change the future was only increasing premiums and higher deductibles for the company and our teams.

We were persistent in dealing with the issues that arose, always keeping in mind that we were doing this for our team members. At the time there was no guarantee company costs would decrease. With relentless caring for our teams at the forefront, those first years we bent the rules for deductibles and doctors outside of the new network and picked up the extra costs billed to team members.

Today we see the financial and healthcare benefits for our team members and their families because we took the risks in the beginning. And we would do it again. Our teams are there for us, and we are there for them. Relentless caring makes the difference.

COMPENSATION: CASH AND OTHER THINGS

Getting the people part of the equation right also means providing fair and equitable wages. That's a given. Fair compensation is not about cutting corners or overloading your teams. Even if your organization is strapped for cash, your people—not you—are your most valuable commodity. They are your business and should be rewarded appropriately.

The Right Amount

Appropriate compensation is personal and on a case-by-case, organization-by-organization basis. Again, keep in mind that you get what you pay for.

I've always believed in compensating people for what they bring to the equation. That can mean base pay; bonuses based on performance; stock options and a stock purchase program if applicable and yours is a public company; a 401(k) retirement plan with a matching contributions program; and a top health insurance plan that is affordable. I also think a team member should have the opportunity to not limit their earnings based on seniority or a job pay scale, but rather their contributions. That's whether a person is a technician, line team member, or a store manager.

Unfortunately, not many companies think that way. They don't reward their team members across and up and down the board like MarineMax. Usually it's only the leaders, managers, and top sales agents that are eligible for extra incentives.

MarineMax, in contrast, has a bonus program for its technicians based on a person's efficiency. It's not about pitting people against each other; it's grounded in the belief that not everyone works at the same pace just because a job is there, so not everyone should be paid the same amount. If you contribute more, you should be rewarded equivalently. That includes compensation, recognition, extra incentives like bonuses, free trips, and more. Again, being open and up front with your expectations and processes and maintaining clear documentation is important to avoid complications.

The Importance of Recognition

Beyond the cash, free trips, and goods, recognition is an essential reward that matters. In fact, recognition is what matters most to team members, according to a recent survey from O.C. Tanner, a global leader in software and services to improve workplace culture through meaningful employee experiences. "Recognize me" far surpassed "pay me more" and "give me a promotion" in the survey—37 percent versus 7 percent and 4 percent, respectively.[18]

Looking at more numbers, Great Place To Work® analyzed 1.7 million responses to its Trust Index™ survey and found that people who felt recognized at work are:

- 2.6 times more likely to think promotions are fair
- 2.2 times more likely to say an organization embraces innovative thinking
- 2 times more likely to say people here are willing to go above and beyond[19]

The Great Place To Work Trust Index Survey utilizes a proprietary For All™ Methodology, which is founded on ensuring consistently positive experiences across all employees through effective leadership, maximizing human potential, and a deep foundation of trust, which in turn lead to improved employee retention, innovation, and financial growth, according to Claire Hastwell, senior content manager, Great Place To Work.[20]

Numbers and methodologies aside, recognizing an individual's contributions to an organization is a cornerstone of relentless caring. And it demonstrates to others that they are valued and that you care.

Since my early days with the Kendall Company, I've worked hard to incorporate recognition into a company's culture. At Kendall, before each shift, team members gathered together to discuss the previous day's accomplishments—recognizing the successes and opportunities—and mark special occasions like birthdays and work anniversaries. As discussed earlier, we do the same thing at MarineMax in our daily stand-up meetings.

All this is just one more way we treat our teams as family and develop relationships and friendships that matter.

Ongoing Coaching and Training

Any one of us can learn something new. In fact, my personal daily goals include to learn something new every day. That's also a part of what keeps people thriving and organizations and their teams growing, developing, and getting better.

Even at small organizations, individual development plans (IDPs, also known as individualized learning plans) for all team members should be an essential part of a culture of relentless caring. These formal plans should include career coaching, goal setting, and continuing education. Being honest and open about individual development is an opportunity for all of us to become better. As Robert Burns, the eighteenth-century Scottish poet and songwriter (think "Auld Lang Syne"), said so perfectly (his words in modernized English), "Oh would some power the gift give us to see ourselves as others see us."[21]

MarineMax has MarineMax University and its online version. The goal of both is to provide team members with the best tools and highest level of working knowledge to ensure the greatest success in the business arenas in which we compete. Not every organization can afford its own university, but with all the online training and learning options—free and low-cost—available today, there's little excuse for not providing your teams with continuing training and education opportunities. Simply google "learning opportunities" or add a specific talent or skill, too, and start your knowledge quest. Of course, do the due diligence on any source or opportunity before you get started with any program.

Industry organizations as well as educational institutions, training facilities, and even product manufacturers generally all have an online presence that organizations can tap to meet their needs. All that's necessary is the commitment to relentlessly care about your teams.

Feedback

In addition to the availability of training and education, continuing feedback is important for team members. Consider a few numbers from Zippia, the career resources organization and website (Zippia.com):

- Organizations that regularly provide employee feedback have a 14.9 percent lower turnover rate than those companies that don't give feedback.
- Four out of ten employees who receive little to no feedback are actively disengaged from their work.
- Sixty-nine percent of employees say they would work harder if they felt their efforts were being recognized through feedback.[22]

I like face-to-face, quarterly performance reviews that are conversation-based and not just numbers on paper (that's in addition to more informal, real-time reviews as issues or problems arise). Again, too few leaders and organizations are willing to invest the time and effort into providing frequent assessments and reviews. But how else can an organization stay on top of what's happening with its team members and continue to maintain its forward momentum?

POST-COVID-19 PANDEMIC WORLD

As the world comes out of the pandemic and learns to live with COVID-19, work, workspaces, and workplaces continue to evolve so that all this that once was optional is now fast becoming table stakes. Workers want more from their employers, their workplaces, and workspaces.

Topping the list is a great culture where they feel a sense of value and belonging, according to a survey by Steelcase. The company designs, manufactures, and partners with others to provide architecture, furniture, and technology solutions in the workspace.[23]

Don't lose sight, either, of the fact that relentless caring for team members across all generations begins with the CEO/president and includes a consistent focus on communicating and surrounding yourself with A players. At the end of the day, everyone wins if team members are in the right job, developing themselves, and enjoying what they are doing and contributing. After all, happy team members mean happy customers.

TAKEAWAYS

- Three of every four hires will not be an A player.
- A C player who shares an organization's values has a better chance of becoming better with coaching than one who does not.
- The real cost of a bad hire is much more than the thousands and tens of thousands of dollars in actual cash expended. It's about how much business that bad hire sends away too.
- The right people in the right jobs are prerequisites to nurture and grow success.
- Commit the time and effort to establish a thorough and well-mapped-out plan for hiring.
- The right kinds of assessment and testing should be essential parts of the hiring process.
- A psychologist on staff, or at least access to one on an affiliation basis, goes a long way toward helping to promote relentless caring and an organization's excellence.
- As with anything else, before bringing in a psychologist,

do your due diligence. All psychologists and coaches are not equal.

- Quality healthcare at an affordable price is a gift to your teams and not a pipe dream.
- To find or put together a top-notch health plan is a challenge but one that even small companies with the right level of commitment can overcome.
- To hire and keep those A players means appropriate compensation. Keep in mind that you get what you pay for.
- Appropriate compensation should include base pay; bonuses based on performance; stock options and a stock purchase program if applicable and yours is a public company; a 401(k) retirement plan with a matching contributions program; and a top health insurance plan that is affordable.
- Personally, I think your teams should have the opportunity to not limit their earnings based on their seniority or a job pay scale, but rather have those earnings be determined by their contributions. That's whether a person is a technician, line team member, or store manager.

Chapter Four

Tenet 2: Stop Talking and Start Active Listening

God gave us two ears and one mouth;
listening is more important than speaking.

Right and real communication is a two-way interaction, the most important part of which isn't talking, but listening. Active and sincere listening. That means great leaders must learn how and when to keep their mouths shut!

Active listening happens when you pay close attention to what is said, understand the message being delivered, and react to it in a thoughtful manner. Following through with the appropriate actions based on what was said matters, too, especially in the workplace, where trust is a huge part of creating long-term relationships among team members as well as clients.

Leaders who relentlessly care about others and how they feel understand that. And they genuinely care about others' ideas, attitudes, and lives.

That's very different from how most people "listen." So often when someone "listens," they aren't really tuned in to what the other person is saying or feeling. Instead, their minds wander; they think about what to say next; they lack empathy and basically don't care what someone else says. They usually interrupt the other person to interject their own ideas. The concept of related questions and follow-through is usually nonexistent.

Remember the discussion in chapter one that linked lack of love or caring in the workplace with the Great Resignation? Workers want culture, connection, and caring, not the "who cares" approach from a typical boss who doesn't listen and could not care less.

This sounds relatively simple, but it's not. Few leaders get it right. Those who do get the concept of being passionate about what they do and listening and guiding conversations to the right conclusions. They understand the importance of individual ownership of problems and solutions to get results. And they understand that solid communication means transparency, which also leads to accountability and trust.

Let's look closer.

WHAT DO YOU REALLY MEAN?

We all have the tendency to speak more than to listen. We tend to jump to conclusions and interrupt without understanding the full meaning of what someone else is saying. Real communication is the opposite.

Active listening is taking the time to not speak and allow the other person to tell their story. Then, the listener asks follow-up questions based on the conversation to bring out the complete meaning and feelings of what the other person really wants to convey.

For example, when a MarineMax sales agent asks a potential customer why she wants a boat, she may respond, "To go to the Bahamas." But does the customer really mean she wants a boat capable of a two-week cruise to the Bahamas? Or could it be that "the Bahamas" is an arbitrary destination, and the potential buyer wants a boat she can use to take trips here and there?

Those are very different needs. No matter the product or service offered, following up with related questioning helps unlock the true meaning of what someone wants to share. Again, don't simply hear the first few words, jump to a conclusion, and then interrupt with your "better way" to do something.

It doesn't matter if you're talking about selling boats or selling cameras, trying to understand a human resource issue, or operating in business or in life. We all must learn to listen to what the other person says in full, repeat what you think someone else said, and then ask follow-up questions. Pay attention not only to the verbal answers but the nonverbal cues—body language—as well.

One of our young daughters is a figure skater. Not long ago, when I picked her up after practice, she got into the car crying. I asked her what was wrong, and she said that she was just sore from tubing on the lake over the weekend. Then I asked her, "How was today's skating lesson?" She responded, "Okay," but from her body language I knew something was off. So, when I returned home, I shared with my wife, Irina, what had happened, and she asked our daughter follow-up questions. It turned out that our daughter's regular figure-skating spins coach had been replaced with someone who taught a different technique. That meant our daughter had to change what she already had practiced and learned. That was the problem stressing her.

Had we not taken the time to actively listen and ask more related questions based on what our daughter said, we would not have truly understood the problem. It's not easy to actively listen, and we all have to work at it. But we can do it if we try. With practice, this kind of active listening becomes habit.

LISTEN TO YOUR CUSTOMERS TOO

Active listening applies externally to customers too. People want to be heard.

I remember one boat show where a couple with their two children was interested in buying a twenty-four-foot cabin boat. They had spent time with our competition but hadn't decided what to buy, so they stopped in to check out our offerings.

As I walked the family around the exhibit, I made sure to engage everyone in the conversation—kids included—and listened intently to what each person wanted and liked or didn't like in a boat. It turned out that when they had visited our competitor, the sales agent was only interested in what the husband said and how soon they could close the deal with him. But I also paid attention to the family's needs. For example, the wife was insistent there be enough electrical outlets on the craft so that she could use convenience appliances, including her hair dryer.

Because we listened and were sensitive to the entire family's needs, the couple ended up buying their boat from us. It was the first of many purchases from MarineMax too. In fact, the family loved our company and boating so much that they became leaders of some of our Getaways!.

That's the story of a single customer who wanted someone to listen. What happens when an organization turns its back on all its customers? It's occurred before! A popular fishing boat manufacturer had a devoted following. Over the years the company nurtured these loyal fans by providing quality products and listening to and passionately caring about their customers. Then the manufacturer was sold. Rather than being honored to carry on the manufacturer's strong tradition of quality and caring, the new buyers' first act was to remove the company's passionate founders. Then they slashed product quality and stopped caring for their customers.

Not long after that, the manufacturer's thousands of loyal customers suddenly evaporated, and boat sales plummeted. Rather than care about its customers, who spoke their minds with their purchases or lack thereof, the company's new owners opted to run the operation with profits top of mind. Where once it was almost impossible to keep these boats in stock, the brand's sales today are almost nonexistent.

Passion for a product/service comes from trust that an organization earns over a long period of time by listening and caring. Violate that trust and, no matter how strong the bond once was, your customers will disappear in an instant, taking their referrals to your company with them.

Over the long haul, you never lose out by taking care of your customers and treating them like part of your family.

ASSESS YOUR LEADERSHIP: ACTIVE LISTENING

Consider the right and the wrong way to actively listen.

The Right Approach:

Sales agent: Welcome to MarineMax. My name is Jim. Can I assist you in looking at our boats?

Customer: Nice meeting you, Jim; I'm Andy and this is my wife, Mary, and our kids, Sam and Patty. [Jim shakes Andy's hand, acknowledging the wife and children too.]

Sales agent: Are you boaters now, and, if so, where do you boat?

Customer: We have a boat on Lake of the Ozarks in Missouri and want a wake boat for our kids.

Sales agent: Great. Sam and Patty, are you excited to get a wake surf boat—and can I show you several of our models? [The sales agent listened to the parents' request to satisfy the children's desire for a wake surf boat, and therefore involved the kids in the selection.]

Customer: Hey, kids, don't be bashful. Let's see if Jim can help us all find the right boat.

The Wrong Approach (picks up after the introductions):

Customer: Yes, we have a boat on Lake of the Ozarks and want a wake boat for our kids.

Sales agent: Andy, you've come to the right dealer as we sell the best available. Let me show you what we have to offer. I am sure that you will be convinced we have what you want.

Customer: The boat is for Sam and Patty.

Sales agent: I understand, but I need to show you the quality and functionality.

THE IMPORTANCE OF SINCERITY

Active listeners are sincere listeners because when you are sincere, you pay attention to more than just the words spoken. That's how I found out what had upset my daughter. I noticed her body language, her actions, and her word delivery.

In business, perhaps a team member is struggling. When asked by their leader if anything is wrong, the person might say, "Nothing." But their body language tells a different story. Active listeners / great leaders don't take the person at their word and walk away. They delve deeper with gently probing statements, including:

- Tell me more.
- Describe to me what's going on.
- How does that make you feel?

Whatever the follow-up, though, don't lose sight of the fact that active listening becomes a dialogue, not a monologue. You must take the time to get more details through verbal and nonverbal clues.

At MarineMax we had a manager who was having difficulty getting several of his team members to listen. The manager and I talked about the issue; I listened to him and kept asking more questions to get to the root of the problem. For example, I asked him how he communicated with his team members, to give me some examples of why he didn't think the communication was working, and how he thought he could make it work.

The problem, it seems, was that the team members didn't respect the manager and therefore never listened to his suggestions. Eventually, with the help of Ray Bowman, our on-staff psychologist whom you'll remember from the last chapter, we identified that the real problem was the manager. He talked a good story but didn't sincerely buy into and therefore communicate the right message. The manager would ask his team to do something that he didn't do or believe in, and the team would ignore his words.

And if *you* don't buy into something and aren't passionate about it, how can you possibly convince someone else to?

In another instance, a new manager at MarineMax had operated his own business before joining our team and was having trouble accepting the idea of working for someone else. He didn't buy into our new basic set of rules because they changed how he had always done things.

This manager even told his team members that team support wanted something done one way, but not to worry about it; do it his way instead. Of course, since he didn't buy into the changes, his team didn't either.

To help solve the challenge, we began coaching the manager about the importance of change and why, as a team player, he needed to embrace that change to sincerely convince others to do so too. Change can be difficult for many people; that's why training and repetitive communication are essential to obtain buy-in.

OWNING THE PROBLEMS AND SOLUTIONS

Over the years and across many situations, I've found the best way to solve many people and performance problems as a leader involves communication that turns the solution into the other person's idea—or at least allows the other person to *think* the solution is their idea. When that happens, the person owns the idea, the solution, and the execution. It's about accountability—more on that later.

Not an Easy Task

You as the leader or manager may not necessarily agree with how someone chooses to approach a particular challenge; that doesn't matter. What matters is that the other person owns it, period.

I try hard to apply this ownership principle to everything I do. Listening quietly is not easy. I have an especially hard time keeping my mouth shut to listen because I want everything urgently done yesterday. But I constantly work to listen quietly anyway both at work and (most of the time) at home.

I meticulously prepare ahead of time for an interaction or discussion on a topic or situation. I continually research possible and plausible solutions and am well prepared before we begin the conversation. But with that kind of knowledge, it's doubly difficult to sit back and let someone else offer an idea or solution. Still, solution ownership is how to make things happen.

I force myself to be open, to listen, and to allow others to lead while carefully trying to direct the conversation via questions that help eliminate unrealistic solutions. It's a delicate balancing act and one that only works if you're committed to it. Allowing someone else to take credit for an idea or course of action is tough too. We all like to be appreciated and admired by others for our suggestions and ideas. But the ability to sit back and relinquish the lead is the mark of a truly great and successful leader.

Not long ago I was discussing a potential MarineMax acquisition with my son, Brett. As the CEO and president of the company, he is ultimately responsible for what MarineMax does. But with my research and experience as previous CEO and now executive chairman of the board, I was confident that I knew what would work and what wouldn't. I still listened quietly to what Brett said anyway.

When I finally spoke, it wasn't to say, "I have a better idea." Rather, I asked Brett what he thought we should do and how he thought we should handle various scenarios. Those scenarios and questions, and his answers, were directing him to conclusions I already believed were the best course of action—though in the process I was open to the possibility that he could have convinced me of a better solution.

When he reached a conclusion—the one I already believed was right entering into the conversation—I said to him, "You're right; sounds like a great idea." And then I added, "Let's discuss your idea more and see if you have any modifications to make it even better."

As soon as I did that, Brett began thinking in the direction I wanted him to, and the course of action became all *his* idea. He owned it; he executed on it; and the success was his.

If his initial course of action hadn't worked, that would have been okay too. We all learn from our failures. Failures, after all, are opportunities to learn and discover positives.

TIPS FOR ACTIVE LISTENING

Up your listening game with the following actions:

- **Be fully present.** That means put down the cell phone, and tune out the distractions externally and internally.
- **Approach the situation with an open mind.** Forget your preconceived conclusions, and hear what's being said.
- **No matter how badly you want to, don't interrupt when someone else is speaking.** It shows a lack of respect for someone else's ideas.
- **Don't fidget or act bored.** We each have the right to deliver our own message.
- **Pay attention to nonverbal cues from the speaker.** That includes body language, eye movements, hand and body positioning, as well as word delivery. Is the person hesitant or are they solid and sure in their delivery? The latter is better. Does the speaker make eye contact? If not, that could mean less veracity in their message. Are their arms comfortable or are they folded in front of them defiantly? The latter shows a combative approach and is a sign that they are not engaged or buying in.
- **Provide the speaker your own cues that you are actively listening.** Nodding your head in agreement and occasionally saying, "Yes" or "That's right," or even the opposite of either, shows that you hear what's being said.

- **When listening to someone, make eye contact with them.** That shows you are paying attention and care about what they say.
- After someone has finished speaking, **ask follow-up questions** to ascertain that you correctly heard what was said.
- Once you understand the message, then you can **ask more follow-up questions to dig deeper** into the issue.

Guiding the Solution

Let's look at another situation, this time with a sales agent whose sales numbers lag behind their peers'. The responsibility of the agent's boss is to communicate that and remedy it. But rather than the boss issuing a typical summons to the office and edict—"Get those numbers up, or you're out"—the best leaders direct the conversation and enable the agent to reach the right conclusion, own the problem, the solution, and the victory.

Done right, that approach creates the all-important buy-in on the part of the team member, meaning there's a greater chance for a successful outcome. Consider the basics of this conversation between a boss and the lagging sales agent—we'll call him James:

Boss: Come on into the office, James. How are Colleen [James's wife] and the kids? Did TJ [James's son] win that baseball tournament last weekend? He's such a power hitter; I can't imagine he didn't hit at least one out of the park. And Anna? [James's daughter] Did she like Camp Kiowa?

The boss begins the conversation with genuine and relentless caring front and center. He asks specifically about James's family members, closely connecting with him because he knows what's happening in James's life. Remember, the entire team is part of the organization's family.

James: Thanks for asking . . . [and he talks a bit about the family].

Boss: How are things on the sales floor? [Both James and the boss know sales are slow, but, again, this is about helping James identify the problem, own it, and then figure out the solution.]

James: Sales have been a bit slow.

Boss: What do you think is the problem?

The boss already knows James has a problem truly listening to what potential customers try to tell him they want and need. As a good leader and communicator, though, the boss wants to help James understand the problem, address the challenge, and invest in the solution. That solution is either upgrade his communication skills or decide that's not possible and recognize that he doesn't belong in sales.

James: I'm not sure what the problem is. We get plenty of traffic [potential customers], but no one seems to be buying. They talk to me, but then pretty quickly leave after I show them one or two things.

Boss: What do you think is prompting those people to leave without buying?

James: You know, I think I'm showing potential customers product that meets their needs, but maybe not. It's like they are not hearing what I'm saying about the features and benefits of a particular product.

Boss: Could it be that you are not really addressing a potential client's boating needs and wants?

James: Maybe I'm not as tuned in to what they say as I thought.

Boss: What do you think will remedy that? How can we help you get better at listening and responding to potential customers' needs? What can we as a company do to help?

James: I'm not sure. Can someone learn to listen better?

Boss: You bet!

James: I like that idea. Do you think I could try it for a bit?

Boss: Why don't I hook you up with a communications specialist who can offer a few suggestions that you can try for a couple of weeks.

James: Sounds great.

Boss: What about we meet again in a week from next Tuesday to review the numbers and talk again? By the way, James, keep up your enthusiasm. Give my regards to Colleen, TJ, and Anna too.

James owns the problem and, with the boss's line of questioning, comes up with the solution: improving his communications skills. Then the boss sets a timeline for improvement and closes the conversation with relentless caring: genuine good wishes for James's family.

This kind of ownership of problems and solutions is all about accountability. Note that the boss didn't start by saying, "I know what's wrong," or "You need to do this." Instead, he listened to what James said, guided the conversation, and let James draw the conclusion that the boss knew would work. This kind of approach works especially well with underperformers. When that person embraces the idea of improved performance with accountability timelines, it's a win-win for everyone.

Again, even if a leader knows up front what the root of a problem is, it's irrelevant. To have even a slight chance of changing someone else's behavior, that person must arrive at any conclusion themselves. They must be part of the process and the solution.

WHEN TO MOVE ON

Let's assume you're great at active listening, genuinely relentlessly care about your team, and do everything possible to help each of them succeed. How do you know when the problem isn't communication but instead that the challenge would be best solved by the team member moving to another job or even another company?

There's no hard-and-fast rule for when to pull back from a situation, cut your losses and your ties, and change direction. When it comes to communication and solving the related challenges with a team member, you must be persistent, fair, and provide the parties involved with the tools and training necessary to make success possible.

To be completely fair, though, if you reach a point where you can't help the other individual, it's incumbent on you as the leader to let that person know it's not working. That's whether you're dealing with a team member or a customer.

ASSESS YOUR LEADERSHIP: CRUCIAL ELEMENTS OF COMMUNICATING

Some topics to remember:

- connect
- listen
- suggest
- direct via questions
- relinquish ownership
- set timeline for solutions

Some questions to consider:

- What do you think is the issue/problem?
- Why?
- How do you think we can solve it?
- What's the first step?
- What's a reasonable timeline to measure results?

TRANSPARENCY AND HONESTY

This type of honesty and transparency is essential for true communication with your teams and your customers. The days of keeping team members guessing or customers at arm's length are in the past. A leader owes it to their team to tell them how they're doing as well as how they compare with other similar operations elsewhere.

Teamwork / Peer Coaching

If someone is doing a good job and better than anyone else, no matter the job or position—entry level to the executive suite—they have a right to know; if not, they have a right to know that, too, along with gaining access to the necessary coaching to help that person get better.

Consider your sales team, for example. Johnny knows Mary's sales surpass everyone else's. With real transparency, her accomplishments should be recognized (verbally and with commensurate compensation), and then everyone—Mary included—should sit down together to figure out what Mary is doing differently and how those methods can be used by everyone to get better too.

This isn't about Mary bragging or being condescending to others or those "others" mocking Mary or making her uncomfortable. This is a tremendous opportunity for growth and improvement across the team. This is peer coaching done right, and it should be ingrained in the culture of an organization. After all, we all want to be successful.

Sharing Successes

We have found that, with the right caring culture, like that at MarineMax, when team members get together, they help each other. They talk about how each can improve on how they do their jobs and boost their performance levels. We apply that same team-effort-to-be-better concept every day at our stand-up meetings in every company location when we debrief the previous day and discuss that day's opportunities and events—and how all of us can help each other do better.

For example, the service team will review the customers expected to come in that day, the deliveries planned, incoming products, and so on. This real communication means everyone in the store knows what's going on; they know who is arriving that day so they can make sure to say, "Hello." And it's genuine, too, because our culture of relentless caring creates a team that's constantly working together to maximize each day's efforts. This isn't a waste of anyone's time; this is a culture of caring from the heart about others and outcomes.

Openness with Customers

That kind of honesty and transparency extends to our customers. If a customer has a problem with one of us or a product, we don't make excuses. We're always honest and transparent, and we don't overlook anything or delay dealing with the problem. After all, a problem only gets worse with time.

Let's say a boat is scheduled for repair on a certain day, and the repairs aren't completed because the technicians were too busy. Instead of making the typical excuse, "The part didn't come in yet," it's incumbent on our team to be honest with the customer. Our typical response is: "I apologize, but our technicians simply couldn't get to the job today. We will be there first thing in the morning to complete the job, and for the inconvenience, we will call you tomorrow to update you on our progress."

Or, if a customer says a team member was perhaps disrespectful or didn't listen, we will apologize to the customer for the inconvenience and immediately offer to set them up with someone else. Then, rather than immediately reprimanding the team member, we will sit down with that person and help *them* figure out what happened and why, determine the solution, and set a timeline for resolution (with more follow-up, of course).

Your "Secrets" Aren't Secrets

Realistically, this kind of honesty and transparency becomes a no-brainer when you consider today's online, constantly connected world. If someone—a team member or a customer—wants to find out something or make something public, it's a few keystrokes or clicks away online, in print, on social media, or somewhere else in the ether.

Long gone are the days when an organization could arbitrarily treat people inconsistently or charge different customers different fees for the same goods or services. If someone wants to know what's happening or the price someone else paid, they can quickly get a good idea.

In our internet-savvy world, very little stays out of the common consciousness; it all winds up online and available to anyone who wants to look for it. Want to know how much a product really costs to make? No problem; google it. Feel like you're underpaid? Still no issue there. Check it out online; even X (formerly known as Twitter) users get in on the dialogue. And if someone doesn't treat you right, everyone will know about that too. Dozens of websites out there can help you; information delivery is big business.

Remember, no matter the size of your organization, as a leader your team and their families and your customers and their families are part of your family. Be honest and transparent with them and care, and in return they will stay by your side like family, through good times and not so good ones. The old saying of "honesty is the best policy" is never wrong.

HOW TO STAY CONNECTED

In business and in life, clear communication is everything. Your team members sharing good news is essential for growth and to ingrain the fact that they are a vital part of a team. In the same way, real and right communication with customers helps break down barriers—especially when problems arise.

If, for example, a promise can't be kept—maybe a service deadline—proactive communication can help avoid confrontation with a disgruntled customer. That proactive communication can be as easy as an email or text. However, though it may sound old-fashioned, nothing is better than a short phone call. Again, making excuses is not the answer; honesty and transparency is: "We apologize that we let you down, and we will work to do better."

At MarineMax we communicate with our team members through an online platform called Jostle. There we share, in real time, birthdays, anniversaries, births of children, promotions, job successes, awards, charity events, team lunches, and any other newsworthy events. This is just one more tool to let everyone know that they are a part of a team that cares about each other. For example, we may announce a new "greeter" at one store, which in turn prompts *welcome-to-the-family* responses from across the country and around the world.

Marketing with Connection

When it comes to ongoing communication with customers, our marketing team keeps in touch via emails that focus on the lifestyle associated with boating. Instead of the typical sale promotions, these emails are about creating emotional connections to boating for our customers based on our mission statement: "We change people's lives" and "unite them on the water." We do that by reminding them of the emotional benefits of boating and how that allows them to connect with family and friends.

This "why" is much more important than how we do it. For

example, from a marketing standpoint, which is a more convincing image: A picture of a big boat on the water or a picture of a family obviously enjoying themselves and having fun as the kids jump off a swim platform into the water with big smiles and laughter? Or even a wake surfer behind a boat with boat passengers cheering them on?

Obviously the last two options deliver where the first falls short. That's communicating the real message that boating is about the experiences it can bring.

TAKEAWAYS

- Leaders must learn to actively listen before speaking.
- Active listening is sincere listening—paying close attention to what's said, understanding the message being delivered, and reacting to it.
- Active listening applies internally to your teams as well as externally with your customers.
- The result of this kind of communication is greater success in terms of the bottom line.
- Successful approaches to fostering the best communication internally and externally include transparency, honesty, and relinquishing ownership of ideas and solutions.
- If someone is doing a better job than anyone else, no matter their job or position—entry level to the executive suite—they have a right to know. Your entire team can benefit, too, from knowing what this team member is doing that they're not.

- If someone isn't performing, they need to know that, too, and get the necessary coaching to help themselves improve.
- Solutions should include timelines for completion or, at the very least, ways to measure progress or lack thereof.
- Forget trying to keep a secret from your teams or your customers. Gone are the days when an organization could arbitrarily treat people inconsistently or charge different customers different fees for the same goods or services. If someone wants to know what's happening or the price someone else paid, they can quickly get a good idea via the internet.
- Find the right communications tool for your teams—one that enables interactive conversations and connections.
- Communicating good news to your teams—individually and as a team—is essential for growth and to drive home that they are a vital part of the team.
- Real and right communication with customers is about openness and honesty, and helps break down barriers, especially when problems arise.
- The best marketing shouldn't dwell on sales promotions but rather on creating emotional connections with your customers.

Chapter Five

Tenet 3:
The Value of Living Your Values

We change people's lives.

—MARINEMAX'S MISSION

Relentless caring is a tall order in the business world, where people generally equate too much caring with weakness and vulnerability. Often, they see a person who is sensitive and caring as a pushover.

Once again, there's plenty of talk about vulnerability and caring. Executives, leaders, and organizations spend hours, weeks, and even months discussing the importance of values—corporate and personal. Not many, though, embody the values they purport to espouse or live them 24/7. It's especially difficult when profits and bottom lines take precedence over long-term relationship building.

BLUEPRINT FOR ACTION

Values are not just slogans on the wall, aspects in corporate literature, or words to be brandished at all-hands meetings. They are the blueprint for actions that are lived day in and day out. To truly practice relentless caring, an organization and its people need to understand what matters—their values—and then live them in all they do personally and professionally. Living one's values is the entry into relentless caring because as someone builds trust with others, those caring actions are viewed for what they are: sincere.

The list of businesses that have gone bankrupt and failed is full of companies whose executives said one thing and did another. Some of the biggest corporate debacles of the last decades—think the collapse of energy giant Enron or communications wonder WorldCom—involved mega corporations that spoke the right words and posted them front and center, but behind the scenes acted out different stories marked by greed, egos, and shady accounting practices.

Consider the common value of honesty. Many people, especially leaders, proclaim the value of honesty, but, through their actions, are not honest in business or their personal lives. Beware of anyone who says, "To be completely honest . . ." or "To be totally honest . . ." Those are red flags that someone is probably lying or at the very least stretching the truth. I have seen that happen over and over through the years, especially with politicians.

Deception-detecting expert Pamela Meyer, author of *Liespotting: Proven Techniques to Detect Deception*, says that people who overemphasize their trustworthiness likely aren't. Some of the words Meyer says should signal caution include:

- "To be honest . . ."
- "To tell you the truth . . ."
- "Believe me."
- "The fact is . . ."[1]

Eye movements and other nonverbal cues are other giveaways of dishonesty. For example, if someone fidgets, changes their tone of voice or speech patterns, starts moving their eyes, or can't focus on you—those can all be indicators that they are not being truthful. As ridiculous as it may sound, when some people lie, they may say "Yes," while shaking their head to indicate *no*, or sometimes cover their mouth or eyes so the person they are speaking with can't see their real reactions.

Foundation for Culture

Values are the foundation for great organizational cultures. At MarineMax, our stated values are honesty, integrity, trust, loyalty, professionalism, consistency, always doing what's right, treating others as we want to be treated, and always considering the long term. These values aren't just words—they embody all that we do. They guide all our actions, and they shape all our relationships with our teams and our customers.

Early on, MarineMax's leaders, managers, and teams spent extensive time talking about what they wanted the company to be and how they wanted to conduct business. This wasn't a time to simply develop a great slogan. Instead, it was establishing how the company's teams would do business—in a way that people mattered both inside and outside the organization.

The MarineMax team was serious about those values because sales alone aren't enough to guarantee long-term success. A team member who delivers results but doesn't exemplify an organization's values, vision, and culture generally doesn't belong in that organization. There are exceptions, of course.

I remember a sales team member—I'll call him Tom—who wasn't honest and played games in the sales process. When Tom described the benefits of a particular boat with potential customers, he would often stretch the truth. Instead of clearly explaining how far a boat could travel on a tank of gas and at what speed, he would say something like, "The boat burns very little fuel. In fact, you can cover four hundred miles on one tank of gas, so no problem with that trip you want to take to the outer islands of the Bahamas."

What Tom left out of that conversation was that, yes, the boat could travel four hundred miles on a tank of gasoline, *but* only at a speed of eight knots (that's just over nine miles per hour). And if in fact the customer tried to travel from Florida to the Bahamas at a speed greater than that without stopping for gas, it could create a serious safety issue.

After hearing a horror story from an unhappy customer who almost did run out of gas and was at risk had they not been discovered by another boater who towed them into port, I asked Tom if he had been clear with the customer on the boat's gas mileage—four hundred miles per tank at a maximum speed of eight knots. He responded, "Yes." But I knew that was an obvious lie by omission. We heard similar comments about Tom stretching the truth with other customers, too, so we dismissed him. Tom's desire to make quick sales and overpromise customers with flimflam sales tactics wasn't living the values that our organization embraces.

Broken Trust

Values, whether we have them or lack them, are huge parts of what make us as well as our organizations who we are. Consider, for example, trustworthiness as a value. Successful organizations are built on the foundation of trust between customers and team members. Violate that trust, and partnerships are destroyed.

A French boat manufacturer—let's call it XYZ Corporation—is an example of what can happen when that trust is violated. One of MarineMax's customers owned an XYZ yacht that had problems and almost sank. We were able to save the yacht, but it required significant repairs to fix the saltwater damage. We evaluated the cause of the problem—a manufacturing defect—and subsequently had the results validated by an independent third-party surveyor. But when we tried to contact XYZ in France, they did not respond because they were closed for their August vacation.

The customer wanted their yacht back, so we took care of the repairs and assumed XYZ would reimburse us for their obvious mistake. When XYZ finally got back to us, they blamed the customer for the problem even though the cause had been independently verified. They also blamed us for repairing the boat without first getting their approval and refused to pay for their mistake.

Eventually—months later and after many meetings with their senior management—XYZ agreed to pay for half the cost of the repairs. That experience taught us XYZ couldn't be trusted to do the right thing, so we subsequently ended our relationship with them. The move cost MarineMax thousands of dollars, but it cost XYZ millions more dollars in future lost opportunities.

Sometimes a leader can misjudge the values of a team member too.

That's a tough lesson I had to learn at MarineMax. Early on we had a great technician. I really liked him; he was outstanding at his job; and I had personally done a lot for his family. I had even loaned them money when they were in a financial pinch.

At the time, our store didn't open on Sundays until around noon, so I usually wasn't there in the morning. This particular Sunday, though, I needed to catch up on some work and decided to go in at 8 AM. When I pulled up to the store, there was my favorite technician loading drums of fuel from the marina into the back of his pickup truck.

If he had asked first, I would have given him the fuel. But he didn't, and it turned out that he had been regularly stealing from the company instead. The moral of the story is: trust your people, but check up on them too. Pay attention to the details.

Leaders Included

A leader must live their values to inspire their followers / team members. One of the original partner companies that made up MarineMax split from us early on because that company's and its leader's values didn't align with our organization. Instead of relentlessly caring about and taking care of customers, that company's business strategy called for hounding manufacturers to get the lowest possible price, turning around and selling products at cut rates, and providing no customer service after a sale.

Because post-sale customer service done right is a big expense in the marine retail business, this company's short-term outlook to maximize profits netted its leader big personal financial rewards. He paid his sales staff handsomely, too, in exchange for the verbal abuse they continually had to take from unhappy and angry customers. His company's lack of customer service was exemplified by the manufacturer's very low customer satisfaction index (CSI) scores.

In the early years of MarineMax, we tried to modify the uncaring culture of this partner and his company. But eventually, before I could even ask the partner to pull out of MarineMax, he did so on his own. He told me MarineMax was a train going clockwise and he was going counterclockwise. Then he resigned. Yes, he was a successful entrepreneur, but didn't share our culture or values.

Sometimes you can modify an organization's culture as we did in the manufacturing business acquisition mentioned in chapter one. And sometimes—as with the partner company above—you just can't. MarineMax eventually had to start over in that specific market with a new team more committed to relentless caring. However, the lessons we learned were invaluable. A few include:

- It's often better to start over than work to no avail to try to correct a bad culture. To change a culture is a long, difficult task that can be expensive.
- Before acquiring any new company, doing your due diligence should include thoroughly researching and understanding its culture and team.

Since that initial faux pas, MarineMax has passed on numerous acquisitions because of poor cultural fit, conflicting values, and the wrong team members.

Individuals who subscribe to a company's values can be coached and trained to excel. Those who don't belong elsewhere. The latter are what the sometimes controversial but definitely successful CEO and author Jack Welch Jr., who led General Electric from 1981 to 2001, called culture killers.[2]

If NPS or other customer service metrics reveal a disturbing or off-value behavior or trend, that should signal a problem that must be addressed immediately. Remember how I talked about the importance of leaders paying attention and actively listening so they know what's happening in their organization? That pertains to living and practicing an organization's values too.

Let's again look at the early years of MarineMax. We had another executive who was successful but very sexist. That's unacceptable, particularly at a public company. This executive wasn't a team player, either, and refused to follow our rules. We tried coaching him; he even worked with Brad Smart as his coach—but he refused to change. Eventually the executive stepped down of his own volition because he realized he wasn't a positive fit for our organization and we weren't going to compromise our culture.

Identifying those people who aren't a culture fit or who don't subscribe to your values is easier if an organization—like MarineMax—has positive and open communication and is relentless in caring about and paying attention to its customer service and customer feedback. Both metrics can be telling signs of a cultural misfit.

Leaders must be involved, listen to what's happening around them, and work hard constantly to be a part of the team. The more involved they are, the greater the insights they glean. And don't forget that it's always crucial to follow up.

THE SECRET TO REINFORCING COMPANY VALUES

Keeping an organization's values front and center is essential, period. As with other aspects of culture, that means reinforcing company values through repetition and reinforcement by modeling the behavior to create a habit and eventually ingrain that habit as part of the culture. At the heart, it's about communication.

In MarineMax's daily virtual or in-person stand-up meetings, managers and their teams review a different value each day. Again, that may sound like overkill. But spending a few minutes daily involving our team moves the value from a rule or a dictum to a habit and eventually to part of our culture as we repeat and repeat the importance of living our values.

These meetings are standard operating procedure in all our locations. Our people huddle every morning to address the day, similar to a sports team huddling to plan strategy before a game or competition.

Over time, this working together as a team becomes habit and eventually a part of the culture. These informal meetings come with a formal agenda that's strictly followed:

- Review and proactively brainstorm about our mission and/or one of our stated company values.
- Celebrate the day's birthdays, anniversaries, and other special events.
- Review the NPS survey results from the previous day and celebrate related victories (remember, NPS is how MarineMax measures customer satisfaction).
- Share successes and opportunities—financial metrics, for example.
- Debrief about the previous day's interactions.
- Address action items for the day and the opportunities ahead.

With the final bullet point, a manager may talk about customers who are due in that day for service or delivery of product. After all, each interaction creates an opportunity to reinforce either a value or a relationship.

MarineMax also further reinforces our values regularly through our electronic communications with team members and our online communications / people engagement tool, Jostle, which I mentioned in the last chapter. There are a number of other communications options out there, including Slack, Microsoft 365 (including SharePoint Online), Adobe Document Cloud, Google Workspace, and more.[3]

Team support sends out the stand-up meeting agenda, which includes content related to a particular company value or mission statement, every day. (See box.) That agenda provides national content as well as a relevant discussion points related to the value of the day to help managers and dealerships emphasize different aspects of the value.

Once again, this is an organized, concerted effort by the company to effect positive behavior change through repetition, which creates habits and ultimately becomes culture. And it works. MarineMax is a company known worldwide for its people/customer-oriented culture and service.

REINFORCING COMPANY VALUES AND THE MISSION STATEMENT

MarineMax helps its teams embrace company values 24/7 by reinforcing those values through regular daily discussions. Here is an example of one day's values-related content that team support regularly suggests to dealership managers.

On Trust:

- **National content:** We are more than a boat dealer. Yes, we sell boats, but we are also a resource. Our customers get access to people with a wealth of experience who can match them with the perfect boat from our unparalleled diversity of brands and models. We provide world-class service, financing and insurance, educational programs, and access to Getaways! trips and other boaters.

- **Quotation:** "Believe you can and you're halfway there." —Theodore Roosevelt[4]

On Integrity:

- **National content:** People who rebound from adversity begin by believing they are capable of finding a way forward. You must have self-confidence and a strong belief in your capabilities to overcome difficult times. You must be open-minded and willing to leverage your talent, know-how, and ingenuity to overcome adversity.
- **Quotation:** "Prosperity tries the fortunate, adversity the great." —Rose Kennedy[5]

On Loyalty:

- **National content:** We all work hard to gain the loyalty of our customers because we know it has value, usually in the form of repeat business. Team member loyalty is also very valuable. A loyal team member is devoted to the success of MarineMax and believes being part of the team is in their best interest.

- **Quotation:** "Coming together is a beginning. Keeping together is progress. Working together is success." —Henry Ford[6]

On Consistency:

- **National content:** Eye contact is one of the most genuine, universal forms of communication. Making eye contact shows you have interest in a person and they are important to you. The supermarket chain Publix trains their teams to make eye contact with customers with every communication. It's a very important part of their culture. What are some of the positive effects you have noticed when you are sure to make eye contact with your customers?
- **Quotation:** "Getting an audience is hard. Sustaining an audience is hard. It demands a consistency of thought, of purpose, and of action over a long period of time." —Bruce Springsteen[7]

On Treating Others as You Want to Be Treated:

- **National content:** When talking to our customers, don't use negative language; focus on using positive language. Instead of saying, "That boat won't be here until next month," try saying, "The boat of your dreams will be arriving here next month." Instead of saying, "We are ten days out for a service call," try, "We can get to your boat in ten days." Better yet, use an exact date or date range. (Talk about other examples you come across every day in your stand-up meetings.)

- **Quotation:** "Do right. Do your best. Treat others as you want to be treated." —Lou Holtz[8]

On Always Considering the Long Term:

- **National content:** Recently Galeon Yachts opened its factory for a tour to celebrate their fortieth anniversary. Share this short video with your team in your stand-up meeting today. It shows the beautiful Galeon factory in Gdańsk, Poland. Notice the state-of-the-art technology and craftsmanship at Galeon. Our relationship with Galeon has been an important part of our growth over the past several years.
- **Quotation:** "We keep moving forward, opening new doors, and doing new things, because we're curious and curiosity keeps leading us down new paths." —Walt Disney[9]

On the Mission Statement *(to provide the world's best pleasure boating experience by consistently exceeding the greatest expectations of our customers, our team members, and our shareholders)*:

- **National Content:** In today's stand-up meeting, please share the message from our CEO, Brett McGill, posted on Jostle yesterday:

The original vision for MarineMax was to create a better customer experience by building a team dedicated to the passion and lifestyle of the boating community. This is the basis of the success of our model, and you continue to work hard to deliver. Thank you for the excellent execution!

Here's a snapshot of our accomplishments this quarter:

- Maintained world-class fans (NPS) scores, currently at 83.86
- A record June quarter revenue totaling $688.5 million

Let's continue living our mission and values and wrap up our fiscal year with a record fourth quarter. Great job!

- **Quotation:** "Never doubt that a small group of thoughtful, committed citizens can change the world: indeed, it's the only thing that ever has." —Margaret Mead[10]
- **More National Content:** For this week's WOW Wednesday and to kick off the 2022 Service Manager meeting, we would like to recognize the entire service team for its commitment to delivering and maintaining the world's best pleasure boating experience! Please share this video with your entire team. Thank you for all you do! (www.youtube.com/watch?v=8lxn8qgm9b4)

- **Quotation:** "No matter what your ability is, effort is what ignites that ability and turns it into accomplishment." —Carol Dweck[11]

IT'S YOUR OPPORTUNITY

Now it's you and your organization's turn to shine, to lay the groundwork for a values-oriented culture that differentiates you from the competition. This will help you and your company stand out and set the stage for being positive and caring toward your teams, your customers, and your community. All that sets you and your organization up for long-term success.

Buy-In from the Ground Up

For any culture and any value adoption to succeed across the board, there must be collaboration and buy-in not just from the C-suite but from all the parties involved. Remember earlier when I talked about change and the importance of relinquishing ownership of ideas as a positive approach for turning those ideas into reality? It's the same when it comes to laying out an organization's values and mission statement.

The most important aspect of determining the success of those values and mission is that your teams feel as if they are contributing to the outcome. With that collaboration comes buy-in. And when everyone takes ownership, the ability to execute becomes far greater than if you handed someone a list of items and told them, "Do it."

Swarm-and-Tally Approach

A bonus of this swarm-and-tally all-hands participation is the advantage of swarm, or collective, knowledge. An organization that invites broad participation in determining an outcome has found the pathway for what is likely to be an enhanced solution. In other words, more participants bring more and different perspectives and ideas into the discussion, which in turn generally leads to a better solution.

MarineMax uses a swarm-and-tally approach when making group decisions around things like mission, values, and "how to get to yes" strategy sessions. It's an approach that can be applied to most any challenge.

First, assemble your entire group to introduce the challenge or problem, then break everyone into smaller groups that are more conducive to discussing the challenge and potential solutions. Within each individual group, come to some conclusions by tallying people's responses and identifying the most-mentioned solution or solutions. These are the ideas that then lay the groundwork for group consensus. Once you've reached a consensus in the small groups, return to the big group and tally up the individual group responses. What are the similarities and the differences? Is there one solution to the challenge that all the groups agree on? If not, then perhaps reconvene the smaller groups to discuss the favored solutions, and keep repeating the process until you reach a solution amenable to all the groups.

For example, let's consider identifying the values that matter to an organization. First, present the challenge to your entire team—what are the values that should matter to our organization? Then, break the team into small groups—perhaps four to six people each—to talk about the individual values that each person feels are important. Every group should designate a moderator to record or write down all the values discussed and emphasize those values that are repeatedly mentioned as important. Each group should come up with eight to ten values to live by and that customers, vendors, and team members expect.

If you're not sure how to begin the discussion, google "company values" or look up definitions of various potential values in the dictionary and discuss them. Almost every organization will want to include values like honesty and integrity. The former is about telling the truth, while the latter is about how someone lives their values.

Other possible values to consider include collaboration, humility, accountability, persistence, or even fun. The goal is to identify the values that matter to individuals as well as to the organization. When considering potential values, some questions to consider include:

- What does the company stand for?
- Is there a particular value that typifies company interactions or the product/service?
- Is there a specific value that the company expects from its team members?
- What values do customers and friends expect?
- What values should never be compromised?

Be sure that something under consideration is actually a value. When MarineMax was deciding on our values to live by, at one point we had about twenty-five ideas—but some actually weren't values. For example, one suggestion was "exaggerate to convince customers and make the sale." That's not a value and isn't in line with the MarineMax culture of honesty and considering what is best for the customer.

After discussion, discard those values that aren't as relevant to the organization or the team. Once the individual groups reach their consensus, compare the different groups' results and repeat the process of flagging the most commonly mentioned values and discarding those that are less popular.

Keep in mind that this is a process and may have to be repeated several times. But by investing this kind of time and effort, the consensus will be just that, and the buy-in will be across the board.

Values that are important to an organization and its people figure into an organization's mission statement too. The mission statement should be a short and concise one-sentence description of an organization's purpose.

With a mission statement, look beyond the obvious. For example, with MarineMax the obvious is "to sell boats." But that's not really a mission statement that can function as the true north for all that the company and its teams do.

The real MarineMax mission statement—"We change people's lives through the lifestyle of boating"—goes well beyond selling and servicing boats. But it is a clear statement of the purpose of the organization: to help change people's lives through boating.

Take the Time and Think Deeply

To identify your organization's mission statement requires the same swarm-and-tally process as is used when identifying values that matter. Again, it can be a cumbersome process, but the results are well worth the investment.

Let's look at some major organizations' mission statements to get a better idea of how to think about your own organization's purpose:

- TED: To "spread ideas, foster community and create impact."[12]
- Amazon: "To be Earth's most customer-centric company."[13]

- Microsoft: "To empower every person and every organization on the planet to achieve more."[14]
- OpenAI: "To ensure that artificial general intelligence benefits all of humanity."[15]
- Google: "To organize the world's information and make it universally accessible and useful."[16]

Some tips to consider when discussing your organization's possible mission statement include:

- Think about why your organization exists.
- What is the big picture—the greater purpose of your organization?
- Be short and concise.
- Avoid jargon.
- Bring in as many opinions as possible—and listen to them.
- Ask if something can be incorporated into the culture of the organization.

Though an organization's values likely won't change too much over the years, often mission statements shift as an organization grows and evolves. It's generally a good idea to review the mission statement every three or four years.

MarineMax started out as marine dealerships that primarily sold and serviced boats. But over the years we've expanded into yachts, yachting, manufacturing, marina management, and travel, so we've tweaked our mission statement slightly. After all, the goal of the mission statement is to lay out how we can provide the best possible experience for our teams, our customers, and our customers' customers.

An organization also may want to consider reviewing its values occasionally, especially if it has grown or changed team members or ownership.

TAKEAWAYS

- Values are what truly matters, whether they're personal or organizational. They are who you are.
- Values lay the foundation for everything a person or an organization does, day in and day out, 24/7.
- Values are the foundation for great organizational culture.
- To keep an organization's values front and center requires repetition and reinforcement as well as for leaders to model the behavior in all that they do.
- The swarm-and-tally approach to selecting values that matter allows for greater input across the board and results in better adoption and execution.
- A mission statement is one sentence that lays out an organization's purpose and is the guide for all that the company and its people do.
- Organizations should periodically review their values and even mission statements, especially if there has been growth and change or new ownership.

Chapter Six

Tenet 4: Make Sure Your People Understand Their Accountability

From every problem there are opportunities
if you just look.

Accountability is essential.

I'm not talking about a military-like approach to holding people accountable where you embrace everything you're told—every dictum—or you're out. Unfortunately, though, too many companies follow that strict approach. Even in today's hybrid or work-from-home environment, some leaders and organizations set unbendable rules that mean that if someone doesn't like or conform to them, they're out of a job.

Delivering on promises and being held accountable for our actions begins in childhood and should be part of every job today, whether someone is sweeping floors, delivering metrics of financial performance, or leading a multinational corporation.

Growing up on a farm in Tennessee, I learned at a young age the importance of accountability. In addition to the farm, my dad owned a business in Nashville that took up a lot of his time while my mom took care of the kids, tended our garden, and canned vegetables.

Author, right, with a childhood friend, growing up on a farm in rural Tennessee.

I was responsible for a range of chores, from feeding the animals to milking cows, and other farm work. And I learned back then that consequences occur when we don't meet expectations. If, for example, I was too lazy to figure out how to fix a broken hay-baling machine before the rain came, the hay would lie rotting in the field and I would face my parents' ire. I appreciate these lessons still today, especially the lesson that there is no substitute for hard work and being held accountable.

THE POWER OF METRICS

As on the farm, true accountability in business starts with defining and understanding the realistic metrics used to measure the performance of people or an organization. The best organizations make sure everyone knows up front what's expected. With those expectations clearly stated from the beginning, measuring up (or not) is transparent and observable in real time. Everyone knows the standard and there's no question about it.

When managers are held accountable and what's expected is spelled out, they can't pass the blame down or up the line. Team members can't pass the buck either when performance metrics are front and center. Too often that buck passing is standard operating procedure in organizations of all sizes and industries. In fact, one oft-cited study found that almost one of every two managers has trouble demanding accountability from their teams.[1] The study from Greensboro, North Carolina–based leadership experts Darren Overfield and Rob Kaiser says the problem ties back to managers who lack the courage to demand accountability from themselves and their teams.

That's not the case, however, with the relentless caring approach to accountability. This isn't about placing blame or withholding information; it's just the opposite. When an organization is transparent with its communications, including company and personal performance metrics, people become accountable for their own actions.

When managers see performance numbers from others in similar situations—sales numbers from a store in a similar environment, for example—they become empowered to hold themselves accountable to produce comparable numbers and expectations. The same holds true with team members. After all, how can you hold someone accountable if they don't know or understand exactly what's expected ahead of time?

Remember the concept of owning the problem and the solution from chapter four? This is it in action in real time. With communications and metrics in place, an organization usually doesn't have to fire an underperforming team member. Instead, that person recognizes they don't measure up and leaves of their own volition. That may sound like a pipe dream; after all, no one likes to have to terminate someone and the idea that we'd never have to sounds too good to be true. But this is reality in an organization with a culture of relentless caring that permeates all levels and all actions. That kind of caring means helping an underperforming team member do better, change roles, or find a new job in which they can succeed.

WORLD CLASS!

MarineMax is living proof of the power of metrics. Utilized right, day in and day out, year after year, they work. As introduced in chapter one, MarineMax uses NPS results as one of our performance metrics. That's how the company knows our customers' level of satisfaction with who the company is, how we interact, and how our teams do or do not serve customers' needs.

Also (though mentioned earlier, it's worth repeating), NPS involves only two questions asked of the customer after every interaction:

1. How would you recommend our company to a friend or associate on a scale of 0 to 10 with 10 the best?
2. Why did you give our company that score? (Of note, unlike other approaches to gaining feedback—for example, why didn't you give us a higher score—our question is unbiased and doesn't make a customer feel uncomfortable for being honest.)

The way people answer the questions helps us break responses down further as follows:

- **Promoters:** If someone gives the company a score of 9 or 10, they are solidly a customer and offer the company the potential of good profits.
- **Passives:** If someone gives a score of 7 or 8, that indicates that they're a customer who can easily be lost to the competition.
- **Detractors:** If someone gives a score of 0–6, that indicates there's a very low chance they'll return to do business with the company and that potentially they provide no opportunity for profits.

Those scores in turn convert to percentages as a measure of performance. At this writing, MarineMax's NPS average for first-year experience with the company is near the 85th percentile (84.6 percent). Over time, as is typical with any company, those numbers tend to drop off, but even after five years with MarineMax, the customer average NPS for all of our company stores is still 65.5. Those are world-class/best-in-class performance numbers, according to the bestseller *The Ultimate Question* by Fred Reichheld, which explores the power of NPS numbers. (MarineMax is very proud of our team's efforts and focus on doing what is best for the customer.)

To put those numbers in perspective, an NPS can be anywhere from a negative 100 to a positive 100. Average NPS numbers vary vastly, but according to Retently.com, which tracks industry average NPS numbers, "A score between 0 and 30 is a good range. An NPS above 30 indicates a company is doing great and has far more happy customers than unhappy ones."[2]

MORE ON NPS SCORES

According to Retently.com, which tracks NPS numbers:

- A score of 0–30 is a good range.
- A score above 30 indicates an organization is doing great and has far more happy customers than unhappy ones.
- A score greater than 70 means customers love an organization and the company is generating lots of positive word-of-mouth referrals.
- The higher the NPS score, the more likely customer referrals will convert into new leads and thus more revenue.

Source: www.retently.com/blog/good-net-promoter-score/.

YOUR CHOICE OF METRICS

An organization can choose from many different performance metrics. Some of those metrics rely on profit margins or revenues compared with expenses. Others count on a CSI—customer satisfaction index.

I find the latter survey approach includes too many questions for customers to answer—most abandon the survey after about the fifth question unless they have had a very bad experience. When MarineMax tried using a CSI, the questions included pertained to product manufacturers as opposed to dealer performance. Another issue with a

CSI in general is that often dealers ask, beg, or threaten customers to get them to rate the dealership at a 10, rather than how the customer really sees the dealer's performance.

Plus, a CSI can be misleading. We had two manufacturers that produced problematic products. When we followed up with a CSI, the customers rated the product poorly, and as an extension of that, the dealership's customer service likewise, despite the real problem being the product, not the service.

In the same vein, with a CSI, if there's a problem-free product, a customer—and therefore the dealer they dealt with—never realizes how good a job was done by the dealership. (On the other hand, with NPS, it isn't about how much someone likes or dislikes a product. We believe it specifically measures the dealership's and its team's performance.)

Adding to the problem with CSIs, often organizations will offer a customer completing a CSI discounts or freebies. That doesn't produce a clear measure of performance and instead skews results. To get an honest performance metric, an organization should never pay for or "bribe" customers for their response. A free oil change or entry into a drawing for cash, goods, or services in exchange for doing a survey does *not* provide realistic and valuable feedback on performance. I think it's insulting to even ask a customer for a positive response to a survey.

At MarineMax, we don't beg, threaten, or pay for customers' responses. And the company pays attention to and follows up on those responses. Remember, they're a daily topic of discussion at the regular stand-up meetings at every dealership and location. That's because NPS is built into the MarineMax culture as a real-time measure of happy (or unhappy) customers. For most of the company's teams, a portion of their compensation is linked to NPS scores too.

In addition to utilizing NPS to help maintain happy customers,

MarineMax uses it to measure the happiness of our team members with our company's performance. That's right; we hold the company accountable and we pay attention to the results. Ours, after all, is a relentless caring culture of one big, happy family. The camaraderie and caring are easily evident when you walk into any dealership. Team members are smiling; everyone is addressing each other by name and discussing their families and successes. It's almost like every visit is a survey of the success of the culture.

Those kinds of happy team members, happy customers, and positive bottom lines are possible in any organization. A huge part of that comes from accountability. No matter the approach an organization takes to that accountability, when the metrics are clear up front, managers know when they deliver and can be held accountable if they don't, and team members understand the minimum that's required and how to exceed expectations.

Whatever the approach to accountability, though, it's important to do your due diligence when picking the metric you use. Find out what others think about its accuracy; once you've settled on one, be consistent and relentless in its application.

REVIEWS IN REAL TIME

Real-time reviews of team members are another essential part of accountability in a relentless caring culture. That differs from most organizations where the usual standard is to provide employee reviews every six months or annually. A few may offer feedback on a quarterly basis. But even that review structure usually is too little, too late to be truly constructive.

When someone makes a mistake or does something right, it should be discussed then or immediately after it happens. Otherwise discussion is ineffective, whether you're dealing with accolades or opportunities for improvement.

Real-time reviews are what truly help your teams and your people grow individually and become better at what they do. Think about it. Few people can recall *all* the details and nuances of every event that happened three months, six months, or especially a year ago. That's not a realistic expectation on the part of any organization. And if someone can't remember the details, how can they fully grasp how to modify or change that behavior for the positive?

Reviews must be given in real time and the response must be proactive in terms of coaching and teaching if the goal is achieving accountability. The formula is action, reaction, review, and revise the negative and reinforce the positive. That's how to effect real change.

If an NPS number or other service/performance metric from a customer calls out a team member's behavior or the performance of a team, that's a red flag for an organization and a warning that must be heeded. Address the issue immediately; don't wait for a scheduled performance review. Months later, the behavior that prompted the red flag at the very least likely has been forgotten or, at worst, has become an ingrained behavior that may already have had catastrophic effects on an organization's culture and the bottom line.

If an organization just experienced a great month, its leader and its team should go back and brainstorm why everything clicked and how the team can do even better. That's coaching in real time. Conversely, if the team had a lousy month, take the time to review and discuss what happened, where the team performed well and where it fell short and why, as well as to talk about how everyone working together can fix what misfired.

That's true accountability and coaching for excellence.

FOLLOW-UP COACHING

Individual coaching is essential too. No matter if someone is part of the C-suite or on the customer-facing line, coaching can make the difference between mediocrity and excellence. Again, the success of coaching partially depends on making the individual part of the solution. That person then becomes more accountable for delivering on what's expected.

Consider Anne, who works in finance and insurance at a boat dealership and helps customers finance their purchases and buy extended warranties. Anne wasn't measuring up in that fewer customers were buying her policies compared to her counterparts at similar stores.

When Anne's store manager asked her why her numbers were lower, her answer was consistently that the sales team didn't introduce her to the customers. The sales team, on the other hand, said the problem was Anne's approach to the customers. Rather than trying to help the customers—the relentless caring approach—Anne tried to *sell* them the services.

Anne's manager then reviewed her Caliper Profile and found that Anne may shut down from criticism (or, as Caliper would phrase it, her resiliency was very low). Taking the relentless caring approach to his team member, the manager decided to try to coach Anne to help her solve the problem on her own. In the conversation that ensued, Anne not only addressed the problem with a solid solution, but also suggested a unique and original approach in the process thanks to the communicative leadership of her supervisor.

The solution became Anne's idea; she owned it, and she executed it as a result. Mediocrity became excellence thanks to relentless caring and coaching.

Here's a roundup of the conversation:

Manager: Anne, we have spoken about what can be done to get your finance and insurance numbers up and improve the store's profits and your income as well. Do you have any suggestions or thoughts on how you and the company both can win more?

Anne: As I mentioned before, I struggle to get the proper introductions from the sales team at the time of the sale. They seem to listen, but still they fail to make the introductions.

Manager: I agree that you must have the opportunity to talk to buyers about the benefits you can offer them, like better financing options and extended warranties. Do you *see* the real benefits that you can offer these customers? Does your presentation to the customer focus on those positive benefits prior to presenting the price associated with each benefit?

Anne: I see the benefit, for example, of an extended warranty. What a bargain the cost is up front compared with buying a warranty after the initial coverage period. That's why I focus on the fact that the extended warranty is a bargain. I just need a chance to present to the customer.

Manager: What would you think about presenting the many benefits of the offerings you have to the sales team during the next daily stand-up meeting so they can realize firsthand how you can make their customers even happier without focusing on the price benefit?

Anne: That's a great idea to focus on the benefits rather than the price. I could even role-play with a sales agent acting as a customer to show why financing is a plus compared with just paying cash for the product. The next meeting, I could focus on the benefits of adding an extended warranty.

Manager: Anne, what a great idea! I look forward to meeting next week to hear how it went.

Outcomes Vary

Of course, not every instance of coaching a C player like Anne nets such positive results. As mentioned in chapter three, there will always be a few C players, individuals who truly can't perform up to expected levels. Someone might be in the wrong job; they might not like what they're doing, be experiencing problems at home, or not have the correct level of expertise. Remember the top sales leader who didn't work out as a manager? He was in the wrong job, one not suited to his personality or happiness.

However, in the case of poor performance, it's important that a supervisor provide the expectations up front—the accountability. Then, if someone falls short, give them the chance and the guidance to self-correct. That's what Anne's manager did, with great success.

If someone still can't measure up and chances seem slim that they ever will, a leader should encourage that person to recognize it isn't working and to look for a new job. Remember, change is easier when someone takes ownership of the problem. If the poor performer fails to do that, once their review is formalized, they need to be terminated.

Hopefully, though, if a leader has done their job right—been open, accountable, and clear in their communication—the chances are they won't ever have to fire that person or move them to a different job. Instead, that person will be the first to raise their hand and say they don't fit. With that sales genius, above, he voluntarily stepped aside as a manager and went back to sales, where he still dominates today.

If someone has to leave a company, initially it's not always a quick, happy ending. But the bottom line in almost every case when there's a separation is that eventually that person ends up doing what they like to do rather than staying on, miserable. A C player who moves on benefits themselves as well as the company.

A leader's best approach to ensuring his team's accountability, therefore, is thinking about the following issues:

- What is the job that has to be done?
- What are our expectations associated with how to complete the job?
- What can we do to help in terms of training and tools?
- What's working and what's not?
- How can we address what's not working?
- What is a reasonable time to revisit the issue?
- If the job doesn't work for someone, is there someone else in the company better suited for the job?
- If a team member has all the tools and is not performing or not happy and neither are you, what can the company do to help them move on?

ACCOUNTABILITY APPLIES TO EVERYONE

As I said earlier, accountability must apply across all levels in an organization. Any company can have a beautiful store in a great market, but without a great leader, the store can falter. The team and the customers aren't happy and the store isn't financially successful. Conversely, there can be a marginal store in a marginal location with an A player manager that thrives.

MarineMax had a beautiful, state-of-the-art store in a great location in an outstanding market. Nonetheless, the store vastly underperformed smaller stores in less desirable locations and continued to lose money. After thoroughly studying the situation and the people involved, we discovered that the store's leadership talked a good talk but didn't sincerely live the company's values of caring for their team or the customers. Once we dismissed the store manager and replaced them with an A player, the store's sales began to turn around. Today it's one of our top ten producers, which is further validation that success is more about a leader and their team than the location or the brand of products.

That's why even leaders, including the CEO, need accountability and coaching to be the best they can be and to leverage their individual potential. It's lonely at the top, and a coach is an opportunity for a CEO or senior executives to really talk about how they can improve their managerial skills. That's another reason having a psychologist on staff at an organization, or at least easily accessible, makes so much sense.

At MarineMax there was pushback when we first began to coach the senior team. The typical excuses to avoid coaching included, "I don't need this" or "I'm too busy." Further, some people felt reluctant to open up to our coaches. But, over time, the team began to recognize the value of having quality coaching always available.

I practice what I preach: I'm the executive chairman of the board of a $2 billion conglomerate, yet I have an invaluable coach, Ray Bowman, our on-staff psychologist and senior vice president for talent and team development. Ray has helped provide me guidance to move acquisition processes forward and find common ground in complicated situations.

To those leaders who doubt the value of a coach, try it. Seriously, once you recognize how much a coach can improve your performance and accountability, you will become a convert. Several years ago when

I stepped aside as CEO of MarineMax and became executive chairman of the board, Ray helped me readjust to my new position. Predictably, at first the move was tough because I had been a hands-on leader involved in the day-to-day operations of the organization for twenty-two years. Suddenly I was no longer interacting with managers and teams daily and had to accept that my son, Brett, now was the leader responsible for the company I founded.

Ray helped me to understand that I had a different but just as rewarding role focused on special projects. He also emphasized that my experience made me a valuable asset to Brett and the company, though at the end of the day, Brett is the ultimate leader of the company. It was his turn to share his talents and vision.

With Ray's coaching, Brett and I have adapted well to the changes and without any conflict. Not many CEOs, new or otherwise, have the benefit of being able to regularly and successfully brainstorm and strategize with their predecessors. We each bring our own strengths to the table, and the results speak for themselves. We owe this smooth transition to our on-staff coach and psychologist along with the way our board looked to our Topgrading- and Caliper-like systems to select my successor.

ASSESS YOUR LEADERSHIP: ACCOUNTABILITY

Some thoughts to consider when it comes to your accountability quotient:

- Do realistic metrics exist for your team members?
- Have you defined the A, B, and C players on your team?

- Do you have a coach or mentor available to help you work through challenges?
- Are you open and honest in your team member and personal reviews, and are they in real time?
- Do you care enough for your team and the sub-performing team members to facilitate a change?

FINDING THE RIGHT COACH

Just as a sports team needs a good coach, so do businesspeople. Also, as with sports teams, not all coaches are equally qualified or good at their jobs. Anyone can call themselves a "coach." But not everyone is good at the job or even right for the job.

Finding the best coach for you and your team is a process that starts with your own commitment to the value a good coach can bring to the table. Great mentors often can serve as excellent coaches. Top search firms also may have quality coaches on staff or be able to help locate the right coach for you. Colleges and universities may be able to help with your search, too, as well as reputable master-class organizations.

As with any other quest for a solution to a challenge, start with several potential coaches, and then do your due diligence. Interview those people, research what others say about them, then narrow your list, and make your decision.

However you choose to find a coach, management teams should be the first to work with that coach. They then, along with their coaches, can pass on the wisdom to others. At MarineMax, we teach coaching skills to our managers, and they in turn work with and help their team members become better at what they do and how they do it.

FINDING THE RIGHT COACH

Some things to consider when hunting for the right coach include:

- **Do the values of a potential coach align with yours?** A coach doesn't have to think like you—only share your values.
- **Is the person open and honest?** The last thing someone needs in a coach is someone who only offers praise and agreement for all that you and your organization do.
- **Pay attention to what referrals say about a particular coach's strengths and weaknesses.** If you and a potential coach share the same weaknesses, that person might not be the best fit for you or your organization's needs.
- **Does the person communicate effectively?** Are they clear and concise in helping identify strengths and weaknesses?
- **Is the individual a strategic thinker who can go out of the box for potential solutions?** Remember, if you're not growing and getting better, you're stagnating and falling behind.
- **Can that person instill trust and be empathetic and kind in communications with team members?**

TAKEAWAYS

- Accountability begins with understanding the metrics of what's expected in terms of performance.
- Clear and defined metrics eliminate passing the blame or pleading ignorance.
- The Net Promoter Score system is a clear and unbiased way to measure level of performance.
- To be valuable, reviews should be in real time and the response should be proactive in terms of coaching, teaching, and achieving accountability. It's action, reaction, review, and revise the negative—and reinforce the positive in terms of behavior and approach.
- With clear expectations of performance, nonperformers generally don't even have to be fired; they leave of their own volition.
- In dealing with poor performance, a supervisor should provide the expectations up front—the accountability. Then if someone falls short, give them the chance and enough guidance to self-correct.
- A poor performance could be the result of someone being in the wrong job. It's a manager's responsibility to help determine and fix that.
- Coaching is valuable whether for line team members or C-suite executives, including CEOs.
- Not all coaches are created equal. Take your time and do your due diligence to find the right coach for your needs.

Chapter Seven

Tenet 5: Be Relentlessly Persistent

There is no substitute for hard work and determination.

—A LESSON LEARNED IN COLLEGE WHILE TRYING TO "CATCH UP" WITH FELLOW STUDENTS' PROWESS IN MATHEMATICS

Challenges are opportunities. We must learn to run toward them. Too often in the face of a problem, people give up rather than address the challenge head-on. But the bottom-line secret to success is to be relentless in your kindness and persistence, and never give up. Even if you lose, it's a win because failures are part of the journey to success. With each failure, you can learn, grow, and become better.

For those who doubt the power of relentless persistence, consider that Howard Schultz had a vision to bring the ambience and flavor of Italian coffeehouses to the United States, yet potential investors rejected his proposal 217 times.[1] That proposal became Starbucks, which today has approximately 34,000 stores worldwide.[2]

Or think about a few words of wisdom from Ray Kroc, who transformed McDonald's into a household name. When the former milkshake machine salesman was asked how he created a restaurant business and become an overnight success at the age of fifty-two, Kroc said, "I was an overnight success alright, but 30 years is a long, long night."[3]

THE POWER OF FAILS

> Failure is perhaps the most important learning/growing tool.
>
> —ASSOCIATION OF PUBLIC AND LAND GRANT UNIVERSITIES[4]

I've had many failures and likely will have many more. Each was a learning experience that has led to my many successes personally and professionally. Yet it's tough for me to remember the failures. That's because once I learn from them—what I should have done differently and how to avoid repeating them—I forget the failure and the negative feelings associated with it and move on. Moving on is essential because dwelling on a failure becomes counterproductive and can continue to haunt you and hamper your ability to use it as an opportunity to learn and become better.

Some of my business-related mistakes have been more costly than others. But failures never stop me, and they shouldn't stop you from growing and improving either.

IPO Pros and Cons

Before the creation of MarineMax, a Houston-based capital group invited my then company, Gulfwind Marine, to participate in an initial public offering that combined several independent boat dealers. The Houston company already had chosen the private boat dealerships to participate (Gulfwind included), hired investment bankers, named a CEO and CFO of the company-to-be, and invested more than $1 million in preparation for the IPO.

At the time, I knew little about public companies. I had, however, thought about combining Gulfwind Marine with several other successful dealers to derive synergistic benefits from one big company. But I was hesitant because I wasn't sure how to do so successfully with the different company valuations and cultures and the diverse personalities involved.

I liked the idea of combining several companies through an IPO, and so did the other companies. They chose me as president, and I named the company MarineMax. Though our new company hadn't yet signed a contract with the Houston firm, we opted to explore the IPO idea with them.

Silence Is a Mistake

On the advice of the Houston group, though, we did not tell our major manufacturer/supplier, Brunswick Corporation, about our new company's intentions to combine and go public through an IPO. I pushed the Houston company to allow us to tell Brunswick because of our close friendships and business relationships with the people and the company. But the Houston capital group insisted that we keep our intentions confidential.

After numerous meetings with the Houston team, we realized their goal was to drive short-term profits and boost the stock at the expense of our new company's culture and values, so we opted to proceed with the IPO without them. In a twist of fate, that same day, before I could call Brunswick to explain what was happening, Brunswick's CEO called and asked me if we were in the process of an IPO. I answered him honestly, sharing that we had just ended discussions with the Houston firm that day. I also told him I was in the process of calling the head of Sea Ray, a part of Brunswick Boat Group / Brunswick Corporation, to explain everything.

His response was, "Oh, sure!" He didn't believe me and was frustrated and angry that we had kept him and the rest of Brunswick in the dark about our plans. The reaction from his team was just as dismal, made worse because the Brunswick strategy focused on a push-pull model and control of their dealers, as opposed to our new customer-centric approach.

William H. McGill Jr., second from right, at the New York Stock Exchange on June 4, 1998, after MarineMax went public.

William H. McGill Jr., center, with his son, Brett, second from left, now the company's CEO, along with other MarineMax team members, ringing the bell at the New York Stock Exchange to celebrate the twentieth anniversary of the company's IPO.

Over the next months, as we proceeded with the IPO, we tried to mend our relationship with Brunswick. Adding to the problem was that we as dealers had personal service contracts in our written agreements with Brunswick that required their approval in change-of-control decisions as well as cancellation rights of brand representation. In other words, we couldn't do what we were trying to do—the IPO—without Brunswick's approval.

Ultimately, after many meetings, Brunswick did approve us moving forward, but only after we paid them $15 million and signed new dealer agreements with certain restrictive rights. Not being open and honest with Brunswick was a costly mistake. It also took years to repair the relationship. That's a mistake I definitely learned from and have not allowed to happen again.

No matter the organization or people involved, confidentiality is important, but people relationships are more important in most cases. The bottom line is that not being totally honest up front cost the newly minted MarineMax $15 million. That was money we could have invested in our new and growing company, our teams, and our customer service.

Costly Mistake

Not doing the right thing always will cost you more than doing the right thing—not just in dollars and cents, but also in damage to your reputation and standing. One of the most common instances of that happens all the time with all types and sizes of businesses: a team member, who hasn't responded to coaching, continues to underperform and their manager drags their feet on replacing them. The result is not just more financial losses, because leaving that underperformer in a job that doesn't work for them or their organization actually does a disservice to that team member. When a team member isn't performing after repeated efforts to help them, a manager must learn to pull the trigger quickly—to either reassign or sever ties with that person pronto.

A sales agent in the wrong position costs sales you may never recoup; a technician who doesn't fix things properly damages relationships. Even a receptionist with the wrong attitude turns away many more potential customers than you'll ever realize.

WHAT IS TRUE PERSISTENCE?

Don't make excuses; just do it!

"If you really want to do something, you'll find a way. If you don't, you'll find an excuse." Those are wise words from U.S. entrepreneur, speaker, and business philosopher Jim Rohn.[5] In other words, if you want to accomplish something, you will be relentlessly persistent and figure out how to achieve it.

Of course, there is a difference between being truly persistent and simply irritating everyone around you with repetition. First, persistence is *not* repeating the same tired phrase over and over. The differentiator is substance.

Persistent: determined to do something despite difficulties, especially when other people are against you and think that you are being annoying or unreasonable.[6]

Add Value

Closely linked to the right kind of persistence is value. Don't waste people's time bothering them unless your persistence is based on solid research on how to add value to something.

Being persistent with facts based on solid research and presented in a kind and caring manner, coupled with listening for feedback, never becomes too much. As I've mentioned, at MarineMax we repeat our values daily *and* involve others in discussions, all with no complaints. On the other hand, if we didn't involve the group and instead preached a value every day, the result likely would be yawning and complaining.

Persistence is essential in the workplace because so often so many people are so quick to say, "No," especially to anything that involves change, says Dorie Clark, author of *Entrepreneurial You*.[7] How true!

It's what someone does and how they do it after they hear the word "no" or face a failure that makes the real difference. Instead of turning away and giving up, relentless persistence requires the courage to believe in your research, ideas, and conclusions. Don't quit; revisit the challenge; review potential solutions and your preferred solution; then figure out how to show the naysayers the value that your solution can bring.

More often than not, if you've been honest (with yourself and others) and thorough, those naysayers will begin to see the light, and eventually you'll win them over. The results will be even better if you've succeeded in getting those naysayers to own part or all of the solution.

Quick Response Is Essential

In another business blunder, this time in 2008 before the markets collapsed, we—me and the MarineMax team—saw signs of slowing ahead. But we didn't respond quickly enough. When the recession hit, we were left with too much inventory for the level of business following the collapse.

We had been too optimistic, believing that "hope" was a strategy, and it proved a costly mistake. But we persisted. We used the experience as a learning opportunity. We learned from our mistakes and created an inventory management system with less inventory on hand at any given moment so that we're not caught in the same situation again. And we haven't been. We learned the lesson well, and it has become ingrained in all our managers.

Even when the COVID-19 lockdown hit, because we had limited inventory in stock, we weren't as concerned with being overwhelmed with product. MarineMax first assured its teams / the MarineMax family that we would take care of them no matter what happened, and we were prepared to do so. Then, as work from home became more the norm, our business mushroomed and worries about inventory or a business downturn evaporated.

BIG GAINS POSSIBLE

Not all challenges end up in fails and losses; sometimes quite the opposite. When MarineMax first began as a public company and started sharing our selling and general administrative expenses breakdown with our board of directors, one of our biggest expenses was Getaways!. I started them through Gulfwind Marine and, with the formation of MarineMax, wanted to grow their operations.

Several board members objected to the costs that, at the time, would cut into the earnings of our newly minted company. Objections were voiced over the high costs for everything from fuel to people, over technicians to handle equipment breakdowns, and over negative feedback if the trips didn't work out.

But in the face of a challenge/objection, the right behavior is to roll up your sleeves and dig in—read: be relentlessly persistent—and I did. I knew that if we continued to commit to doing the trips, we could do a great job. I also knew the trips could create future business for MarineMax because participants would want to trade up to larger boats and would tell their family and friends about their great experiences.

What's more, from listening and paying attention to our managers and customers, I was sure that there was a strong demand for MarineMax-sponsored boat trips. After researching what competition there might be, I recognized that the market wasn't properly served by existing organizations, either, which gave us a competitive advantage.

My research and persistence paid off. In fact, our Getaways! have become one of MarineMax's best marketing tools. Our customers have fun; they make new friends; and inevitably trip participants usually want to buy bigger boats. They want bigger staterooms, faster boats, and more bells and whistles. And they want to explore new destinations. All that has a positive effect on our bottom line.

No matter the situation or the circumstances—business or personal—relentless persistence almost always is the best course of action. Whether you succeed or fail, at the very least you will become a wiser and better person in all that you do.

Persistence has paid off in my personal life too. I'm on my third marriage. My first, to a wonderful woman and mother, lasted twenty years; we had three beautiful children—now adults and parents themselves—and we have nine grandchildren. After our children grew up and went out on their own, my first wife and I amicably decided to go our separate ways.

Not long after my divorce, I married again. The marriage didn't work out because I failed to Topgrade. Before someone balks at the idea of "testing" a potential mate, think about it. Topgrading is a means of understanding the real person, their beliefs and ideals, propensity to act and not, and so much more. In other words, it's just one way—my way—of truly knowing someone. I obviously had not done my homework on understanding both our needs because this second marriage was brief.

But I learned from my mistakes and refused to give up on the institution of marriage. I've been married to my third wife, Irina, for more than eighteen years (more on that in the next chapter). We have two beautiful children and enjoy every day. As I mentioned earlier, before we married, though, Irina took a Caliper test and went through the Topgrading process so we could understand our strengths and weaknesses up front. Today, with two wonderful daughters, we have a great relationship and really do understand our differences and appreciate each other thanks to us both doing our homework in the beginning.

HOW TO PRACTICE PERSISTENCE

Talking about persistence can be lots easier than following through and actually living it. That's especially true when a leader is trying to teach others to do the same thing.

I've made sure to teach my children—my three grown children as well as my two young daughters—that persistence matters. Believe it and live it! A favorite family story involves Brett when he was in high school and responsible for mowing the lawn. On this particular occasion, despite my ongoing reminders, Brett had put off the chore until the grass was tall and thick. One day, I came home from work to find the riding lawn mower sitting in the middle of the front yard with only a small swath of grass cut.

It's important to note that ours was not a new lawn mower, and it turns out that this afternoon the mower had decided to stop moving forward; it would only go in reverse. So, Brett decided he didn't have to finish the lawn. By the time I got home and saw the idle mower, it was getting dark. I went outside anyway and proceeded to mow the entire lawn riding the mower backward holding a flashlight as Brett and the family watched from the window.

Admittedly, the next morning there were a few strips of grass that weren't mowed. But I had made my point on the importance of persistence—where there is a will, there is a way. The family still jokes about the incident today, and they certainly haven't forgotten the lesson learned. That's why some of my family and team still refer to me as a "Scud Missile." (The Scud was a highly inaccurate missile developed by the former Soviet Union during the Cold War.)

TRAITS ASSOCIATED WITH PERSISTENCE

People who are persistent often share certain characteristics, including:

- patience
- the ability to listen
- willingness to accept feedback
- the ability to understand and share their challenges and the facts and benefits associated with them
- willingness to thoroughly research something
- willingness to deviate from a plan if convinced by others based on their thorough research
- the ability to consistently repeat the message
- the ability to never give up

The Three Rs

Beyond the grass mowing event, over the years I have learned how to enhance persistence in myself and others with the help of the three Rs: research, review, and repetition. Research and review means that you should, up front, thoroughly understand the challenge/problem, the players, and the potential solutions. Then, after you determine the best course of action, know that the best way to bring about change in others is repetition. Model the behavior, direct the conversation, and repeatedly show others the benefits of this best course of action until they embrace the solution too.

This sounds like a lot of work and commitment for someone, especially an already overworked leader of an organization, and it is. But as I've written throughout this book, others accept and embrace change more easily and smoothly when they buy into the solution.

An order issued by a leader is a dictum, not an easily embraced solution to a problem. Getting buy-in—or, even better, ownership—of strategies, opportunities, challenges, and career moves facilitates positive outcomes.

That's universal whether in business or your personal life. And in business, if the culture is one of relentless caring, leaders want their teams on board and doing their best. With buy-in, they will be.

THE MODEL FOR PERSISTENCE

To help reinforce your persistence, with each challenge, ask yourself the following questions:

- What is the challenge/problem that needs a solution?
- Who are the players involved?
- What are potential solutions, considering costs and risks?
- What is the best solution?
- How can I model the best solution?
- How can I reinforce this best solution with the players involved?
- How can I persistently reinforce this best solution until others embrace it too?

IN THE PRESENCE OF DOUBT...

Consistent persistence is even harder. After all, doubt is part of human nature and always in the picture. But if you have been thorough in your research and honest with yourself about the pros and cons of a course of action, there's a better chance of overcoming those doubts—both yours and others'. In other words, don't allow tiny doubts to derail what you know is right.

I am the kind of person who, if there is a problem or opportunity, will figuratively throw every conceivable concept up on the wall and see what sticks—what can we do as a solution; what are others doing; what's an easy fix; how can we take it to the next level; what's never been done before; and so on.

That said, however, each of us must be open to actively listening to what others say about a course of action too. And even if someone else hasn't done the research you have, that doesn't mean they might not have a better idea or approach. Sometimes a proposed solution that you absolutely are convinced is a no-brainer ends up not working, while something you doubted the most becomes the biggest success.

Everyone has strengths and weakness, especially leaders. Good leadership is knowing those strengths and weaknesses, and taking steps to learn how to become better, to enhance your strengths and pay attention to and compensate for your weaknesses. Remember, nothing is going to 100 percent work, and everything is subject to change. Whether a process, pricing, product, or something else, nothing is perfect. No one is either. Again, that sounds like a no-brainer, but if that's the case, why don't more people recognize and live it?

My Caliper Profile shows that I always do lots of research before I make a significant decision, and, as a result, it's hard to get me to change my mind. I have learned to force myself to slow down and actively and openly listen to what others say whether that comes in the form of objections, thoughts, or modifications. Without knowing that weakness as revealed by my Caliper Profile and the subsequent coaching I undertook to get better, I am not sure I would know to slow down in that way.

Sometimes, though, I have ideas that I know are right—and they are. A prime example of that is MarineMax's involvement with the Polish yacht manufacturer Galeon Yachts. Several years ago when I suggested the company would be a good fit with ours, my team thought I was crazy to want to team up with a boat manufacturer who was then an unknown in the United States.

But I had seen Galeon's top-quality product, met with its founder, and seen the company's culture, so I was convinced they were the right European partner for MarineMax. I flew to Poland with several members of my team who had questioned that partnership. The trip proved to be an eye-opener. My team quickly saw what I saw, and the partnership became a done deal.

Fast-forward more than seven years, and MarineMax has helped transform Galeon into one of the top-performing brands in the United States. The company builds yachts for us that range in size from thirty feet to eighty feet and are priced from $500,000 to $8 million.

In the face of doubt—yours and/or others'—consider a few questions:

- Did I do enough research?
- Was it the right kind of research?
- Did I put too much emotion into my decision about a course of action?
- What are the chances of success?

And, just because someone still has questions or doubts doesn't mean they should be discouraged from stepping outside of the box (more on the importance of taking calculated risks in the next chapter). The bottom line is to do your research, but listen to others' input and be willing to change your mind.

THE TO-DO LISTS

Another trick to help reinforce relentless persistence is to create daily to-do lists. The lists address what must be accomplished each day. Personally, I divide tasks into three lists:

- What can I do best?
- What can others do, and possibly better?
- What can be delegated?

Whether you're a busy leader like me or an aspiring one, these lists aren't about being fastidious; rather, they are a simple organizational tool to help anyone maintain relentless persistence related to what needs to be done that day and what doesn't and what is the highest and best use of your time and skills—and those of others. The lists also are a great way to not lose sight of short-term and longer-term goals. Keep in mind, too, that you can't always complete everything on your lists every day.

Research has shown that people are more productive when they get rid of or delegate less important tasks and replace them with value-added ones. In fact, a study that appeared in *Harvard Business Review* found that we can free up as much as 20 percent of our workday by simply focusing on what we can do best, what can be delegated, and what we can forget altogether.[8] The wisdom of that course of action is especially evident today because all of us are bombarded daily with so much messaging in so many formats.

I first began making my to-do lists early in my career at Pratt & Whitney to keep track of the minutiae with the various projects I was working on at the same time. Eventually (with repetition), making those lists became a habit and part of the culture built into MarineMax.

Before getting started at work—whether at the office or on the road—I make a list of what I want to achieve that day. That way I also have time to think about the lists before meetings start or the phone begins to ring. Typically, the lists may include things like checking on the status of projects, reviewing key metrics with managers, calling manufacturers, meeting with HR staff about new hires, planning for a business trip, and more.

Next, I review the list and decide which items only I can complete, which ones others can do best, and which ones I can do but could be delegated to save me time. As the day evolves, I refer to the list and add more items as they come up with the understanding that some of the items may have to be moved to a future day's list.

Taking the time to plan the day and document the action items in the plan is critical to executing the plan and completing what needs to be accomplished. When it comes to deciding what belongs on my to-do list versus delegating something to someone else, I focus on my strengths as well as the strengths of others. Just because I *can* do something doesn't mean it belongs on my to-do list. Think about whether someone else can do a better job with the task—perhaps they could be quicker and more efficient at accomplishing the task. For example, I can research something, but is there someone else who already has greater expertise on the topic and better research skills?

Almost every day, my list includes following up on the status of work done by others, so a brief note, a quick visit, or a phone call answers my question on the status of the work. More importantly, reaching out like that shows the other person I care.

The lists can be long in terms of the number of items, but they don't have to be complex or too formal. I try to keep the entries short—a few simple words as opposed to dissertations. Your lists can be a series of notes on a smartphone, written down on physical paper, or even filling out a reusable template on your PC.

There are plenty of free or paid apps you can use too. Some may work better for you than others, so try a few before you settle on any. Even if you have to pay for something, it's well worth it if it helps you stay on task and on track. Or, again, you can always opt for an old-fashioned notepad. In some cases, the latter might even make more sense, especially if a list is long, because it can be gratifying to cross something off the list.

TIPS FOR YOUR TO-DO LISTS

- Make your lists without any distractions.
- Focus, focus, focus on the plan for the day and then work the plan..
- Categorize and delegate to-do items based on who can do the best job on each thing.
- Be flexible and understand the lists may need updating.

I do my lists in the morning or after business hours when there are no distractions and I can really focus on what needs to be done, by whom, and when. The time that you opt to do your lists is a personal choice. The important thing is to do the lists, pay attention to them, and keep updating them. These lists are living and changing constantly. When something is completed, mark it as such. Even if you're swamped that day, crossing something off the list is an accomplishment/reward worth noting, and it's a motivational boost to help you maintain your relentless persistence.

Lists aren't just for top-level executives either. They're a tool anyone can benefit from using to help organize busy days. After all, you can't be organized if you don't have a plan to execute.

Don't allow your lists to discourage or overwhelm you either. Instead, prioritize and re-prioritize. Even the best intentions and schedules get disrupted, so if something doesn't get done one day, move it to the next day's list.

Relentless persistence with your objectives, strategies, and action items, though, goes well beyond making to-do lists. Successful execution involves communications and follow-up with your teams. When you do that, and your teams know and expect it, that's extra motivation for them to get the job done and done right.

ASSESS YOUR LEADERSHIP: SAMPLE LISTS

Consider this sample list from one day in August. Note that the to-do items are short and concise and that I use someone's initials to indicate who should accomplish what (M=me).

To Do:

- **M:** Review the quarter-to-date expenses
- **M:** Call Mark and get update on progress of new model

- **M:** Call Jacek and discuss visit dates to Poland; topics of discussion
- **M:** Congratulate MM and AA on proxy progress
- **M:** Visit team in HR department

To Delegate:

- **MM:** Ask CFO to get more insights into the increase in boat show expenses from budget
- **AC:** Get aged inventory analysis and forecast
- **LC:** Plan travel and arrangements for Poland visit

To Put Off:

- **M:** Discuss with Brett progress on XYZ acquisition
- **RK:** Follow up on hydrogen project

TAKEAWAYS

- Every failure is a learning experience.
- We all make mistakes in business and in life.
- Learn from mistakes, then move on. Dwelling on a past failure is counterproductive.
- Not doing the right thing will always cost you more than doing the right thing—not just in dollars and cents, but also in damage to your reputation and standing.

- Relentless persistence requires the three Rs: research, review, and repetition. Thoroughly understand, up front, the challenge, players, and solutions. Then, after you determine the best course of action, understand that the best way to bring about change in others is repetition. Model the behavior, direct the conversation, and repeatedly show others the benefits of this best course of action.
- No matter how set you are on a course of action, be open and willing to listen to what others say.
- If you have been thorough in your research and honest with yourself about the pros and cons of a course of action, you have a better chance of overcoming personal doubts about that plan.
- Good leaders know their strengths and weaknesses and how to become better by enhancing their strengths and compensating for weaknesses.
- A simple organizational tool to help keep your relentless persistence on track is a daily to-do list.
- To-do lists should be divided into what you do best, what others do best, and what you could do but still can be delegated to save you time.

Chapter Eight

Tenet 6: Without Risk, There's No Reward

Make hay while the sun shines.

—A LESSON FROM GROWING UP ON THE FARM IN TENNESSEE

I believe, 100 percent, that from every problem comes an opportunity. You simply must find it. That's why the courage to take risks is essential to move forward in business and in life.

Whether you're trying to solve a problem or break new ground, if you don't take risks, you jeopardize the future. After all, change done properly ensures growth because in the absence of growth is decay.

What's important to remember about risk, though, is to do your homework before stepping outside your comfort zone. Risk has the power to transform but only when combined with clear research and foresight that keeps the big picture in mind.

Back in those early days of the space race in the 1960s, when President John F. Kennedy told the world we would put a man on the moon by 1970, that was definitely a risk. No question it was out of the comfort zone—ours and the rest of the world's.

Until that time, the longest an American had been in space amounted to fifteen minutes. And then we—myself included—began working on a future space station and putting a man on the moon. Today the goal is again the moon, then Mars and beyond. Just as back then, we have some clues of what might work and what doesn't, and we set out to try the options—to take the risks based on thorough research—that hopefully lead to the rewards.

The rewards can be great. Some of the world's greatest change-making inventions and benefits are a result of the pursuit of man's travel into space. Think of computers, medical imaging techniques, durable healthcare equipment, artificial limbs, water filtration systems, solar panels, firefighting equipment, shock absorbers, air purifiers, home insulation, digital photography, infrared thermometers, information technology, and countless other vital inventions.[1]

A CATALYST FOR PROGRESS

It's the same in business. Take the risk and reap the rewards. That's whether the risk is the result of a problem or part of an effort to blaze new trails. The responsibility of an organization's leaders is to lay the groundwork with the right research and direction.

In entrepreneurship, the approach is referred to as calculated risk-taking, says Rebecca White, PhD, professor of management and the James W. Walter Distinguished Chair of Entrepreneurship at the University of Tampa. Rebecca is also a past president of the United

States Association for Small Business and Entrepreneurship. "Every person, leaders included, makes choices every day, and it is those small choices along the way that make up what we are and have now," she says.

"A good boater checks her engines to make sure the boat is in good order before leaving shore," Rebecca adds. "Regular boat maintenance and care are required, too. It's the same with a leader who takes risks with their company. Calculate the risk, understand it, own it, and then make a decision and move forward, figuring it out as you go along."[2]

Well said.

I always remind myself and our team at MarineMax of a quote from Albert Einstein. "A ship is always safe at the shore, but that is not what it is built for."[3] These words are a reminder that progress is made by taking risks. That's how I approach any problem or challenge.

Einstein also said, "In the middle of every difficulty lies opportunity." All we have to do is look for it.[4] That's a message we at MarineMax repeat over and over to our teams (it's back to repetition→habit→culture). Repetition removes the focus from dwelling on a problem to figuring out how to fix it or to leverage the potential benefits that can come from it. It's all part of a culture based on relentless caring.

If a customer has a problem, whether it's caused by that customer, our company, or the manufacturer, the MarineMax culture leads our teams to run toward the challenge to help solve it. If the problem is the company's fault, we face that head-on too. That's a different tack from many organizations, where passing the buck is standard operating procedure, to the frustration and disappointment of customers and often team members.

Even if a problem was caused by a customer or a product manufacturer, an organization's team should embrace solving the challenge.

As I mentioned at the beginning of chapter six when talking about accountability, in the face of a challenge, true caring is not about casting blame and walking away from being a part of the solution. Just the opposite.

I have always been a risk-taker, albeit I usually explore the impact of what can happen if the undertaking fails before I take the risk. That's probably because I'm an engineer and was raised on a farm, both factors contributing to the fact that I always look at many different possibilities to solve a problem, even possibilities that may create other problems. I remember growing up on the farm, when the hay was in the field and needed to be baled before an impending storm—and the baling machine would break down. I had to find a solution to the problem. Normally that meant using baling wire or a welder for a temporary fix. If one solution didn't work, I would look for another until the job was done. Those early lessons in tenacity continue to prove invaluable with challenges in business.

In the face of a problem, an organization or a team member's first step is to choose whether to be honest with others—customers and/or team members. By now you know I believe that honesty should be built into an organization's culture. But even that comes with risk.

Let's say a technician fails to properly service a boat's engine and the result is engine failure. Does the company hide the error or admit it? Admitting the mistake—being honest—could risk the customer losing trust in the organization's ability to properly service the boat. Or, that honesty could establish a long-lasting trust.

The above situation has happened many times at MarineMax over the years. Each time, we have done the right thing and told the truth, and each time, without exception, the result has been the creation of a trust bond between the company and the customer that has led to repeat and referral business.

Risk Takes Courage

Early in my career, when I decided to leave my corporate job with Kendall and invest everything in launching a boat dealership in Florida, I did my homework, weighed the pros and cons, and decided to jump in feetfirst. It was a calculated risk, and it hasn't always been smooth sailing—it never is—but the risk has paid off. I don't know what would have happened in my career had I not taken the risk, but I do know that, without risk, I would not have grown and learned as much as I have working in one of my passions.

Even the founding of MarineMax was a risk that took courage to implement because the proposed company could (and did) upend an industry. At the time we had the idea of one big company consolidating smaller marine dealerships, the marine retail industry was unsophisticated and very fragmented. There were about five thousand independent smaller dealers worldwide. We knew that our plan to consolidate dealers would likely mean an industry shift, too, from a manufacturer's "push" model to one that is a "pull" model, where the wants and needs of the retail customer take precedence over what the manufacturer wants to produce.

Nonetheless, we took the gamble—and here we are today, the largest and best in our industry for boats and yachts from eleven feet to more than two hundred feet. The company has won multiple awards, too, for everything from customer satisfaction to marketing, design, creativity, sales, and safety.

We've taken many more calculated risks at MarineMax. Getting started in the travel business with our Getaways! boat trips was a risk. So was our foray into the charter catamaran business. With the latter, a number of years ago, I saw an opportunity in an underserved market. From talking to and working with our customers, I knew that many of them were interested in charter catamaran trips. I was also convinced that we could provide our customers an outstanding experience.

Several on our board of directors as well as top managers thought it was too risky a venture, their fears exacerbated by the fact we would be entering a business dominated by several big companies and would need to design and build our own catamarans. But I had done my homework and recognized that we could make it work.

Risk Versus Reward

As I did with the catamaran venture, long before ever implementing any new idea, leaders must weigh the potential risks versus rewards over the long term. The tendency often is to only look at short-term gains/losses associated with something. That doesn't tell the real tale, because change itself can lead to short-term losses. If, for example, an organization buys a company, short-term losses resulting from the initial expense generally are a given unless companies are a culture and market fit.

A good way to weigh the risks and rewards of something is through a formal or informal SWOT analysis. SWOT is an acronym for strengths, weaknesses, opportunities, and threats. Without allowing emotion into the equation, list the pros and cons of whether something can be successful and consider the what-ifs surrounding potential success or failure. SWOT is helpful whether the decision is small or large, individual or company-wide.

If an organization is considering moving or opening a new facility, for example, the physical location in a market could be a strength or, if access to the location is limited, a weakness. With a potential acquisition, if the culture of the company under consideration is misaligned with your company, that's a weakness. Conversely, if the cultures are similar, that's a strength.

When I (or my team) do a SWOT analysis, I also look at whether a potential change will benefit the team, the customers, and even the shareholders. That's important because believing in the success of taking a risk is essential if the effort is to be rewarded.

The ability to convince others to accept risks requires that same belief and commitment. And when you surround yourself with the best and the right team from the get-go, the research and execution of a project—from SWOT analysis to team brainstorming and collaboration—are much easier.

ASSESS YOUR LEADERSHIP: SWOT ANALYSIS

Before making crucial decisions, consider a SWOT analysis of proposed solutions. SWOT is an acronym for:

- strengths
- weaknesses
- opportunities
- threats

With the potential MarineMax foray into the charter catamaran business, as part of my early SWOT analysis, I recognized that I wasn't a catamaran expert—that was a weakness. So, to compensate, I suggested we hire Lex Raas, the ex-CEO of the world's largest charter operator, The Moorings and Sunsail, to lead our project.

(Important note: If an organization or a person opts to take a risk, especially if it's something new or hasn't been done before, leaders and the organization must be honest in terms of their expertise and what their people know and don't know. In turn, they need to bring in the right talent to help and teach others the correct way to do something.)

With Lex's leadership and several of his previous team members onboard, we thoroughly researched what already existed in the charter catamaran space, what worked and what didn't, and the demand, or lack thereof, in the charter travel business.

That kind of due diligence should be standard operating procedure for anyone and any organization *before* going all in on any new and different project, no matter the size of an organization or its industry.

Our research included experiencing the competition's product. Several team members and I chartered a catamaran from one of the leading charter operators at the time and ventured to the British Virgin Islands. That trip helped us see what worked and what didn't, as well as how we could improve the charter experience for our potential customers. A few of the trip's revelations included:

- The sailing catamarans we encountered didn't have their sails up, so we decided we wanted to offer power catamarans rather than sailing ones.
- Water tanks on a boat run dry after a couple of days, and it takes approximately ninety minutes every time to fill the tanks.
- The competition's power catamarans were modified sailboats. That's like trying to make a racing boat from a tugboat.
- Standard propane stoves on the boats are antiquated and a potential safety issue.

To solve the last three problems above, we decided to include diesel generators on our boats that permitted full electric operation, complete with air conditioners and induction cooktops as well as water makers. An added bonus of a generator is the ability to produce hot water, thus eliminating the usual icy showers on the back deck common on most charter boats.

In addition, we experienced firsthand the hassle of securing the boat to a mooring/stationary anchor in the water, where someone must scramble to the boat's bow to grab the mooring. It's cumbersome, so we decided our yachts would have a simple, direct route to the front deck from the flybridge (upper deck) to make mooring easier.

The observations we made on that trip translated into customer-centric features that we designed into our product and which became the DNA of our brand. They differentiate us. We also listened to boat operators on ways to improve the charter process.

We then selected a manufacturing partner to produce the power-designed catamarans and launched the business in the British Virgin Islands. It took more time and relentless persistence to promote and market our brand, train people, and eventually grow the business. But the risk was worth it. Today we have a fleet of power catamarans that operate in the British Virgin Islands and the Bahamas, and reap the ancillary benefits of selling ten different power catamaran models internationally under the Aquila brand. It's a $150 million business with the right team who knows we care for them, our manufacturers, and our customers. And that's not just idle chitchat. Our customers always return from their trips and say, "You're the best."

We *are* better than our competition because of the research we did and continue to do, because we listen to our customers and our operators, and because relentless caring is our culture. It's our advantage in the market.

These are only a few of the calculated risks I've taken in my business career. Each was done after thoroughly researching the possibilities, the market, and the pros and cons, and paying attention to strengths and weaknesses—mine and my teams'. We aren't afraid to admit shortcomings, and we face challenges and bring in the necessary expertise to make up for them. The rewards are worth it.

HOW MUCH RISK IS ACCEPTABLE?

The amount of risk someone is willing to accept is an individual choice and depends on the people, the research, and the commitment to a goal. That's true in business as well as our personal lives.

I am a calculated risk-taker and love taking risks for the rewards and the lessons learned. A great example of that risk-taking is how I met my wife, Irina. It's a long story but indicative of the importance of committing the time to do the research, take risks, maintain persistence in the face of challenges, and reap the rewards as a result.

As I wrote earlier, at the time I met Irina, I was twice divorced with three grown children and nine grandchildren. It was a rainy Sunday in September more than nineteen years ago. My grown kids were otherwise occupied, so I went into the office at 6 AM. When I got there and sat down at my desk, I saw a sticky note on the corner of my desk with a dating website URL that a college engineering buddy had told me about a few months earlier.

At that moment, I thought, *What the heck.* I had been single for a time and hadn't clicked with a number of dates, included those suggested by a professional dating agency. So I clicked on the website and filled out my profile.

I then typed in that I was interested in European women aged thirty to fifty years old. Up popped more than 2,200 women matching my criteria. Never one to be put off by a challenge, I decided that by the end of the day I would narrow the list to ten women. My first pass, I admit, was as a typical sexist male; I narrowed the list to several hundred based on looks. I did more "research" (as in, looking at pictures and reading about the women), and ended up with ten whom I thought might have potential.

As a big fan of the Topgrading hiring and promotion process and its many successes with MarineMax, I decided to create a pseudo-Topgrading interview of my own in the form of an email about myself to send out to these women with specific questions for them too. It included pictures of myself, my kids and grandkids, and honest details about me. As is typical with our Topgrading-based assessments, I included chronological questions that covered areas such as tell me what you enjoy doing, about your childhood, your parents, your schooling, your jobs, your dislikes, your frustrations, your health, and more.

Within the next few weeks, I heard back from all ten women and began narrowing my search based on many emails and their answers to my questions. I eventually narrowed the list down to two women—coincidentally both from Russia—primarily based on their values and beliefs. After more questions and answers and a telephone call, I had decided Irina might be the one.

I did not want to go to Russia, so I suggested we meet in Paris the day after Thanksgiving.

By now, my grown kids and even my father had heard about my new approach to dating via the internet, and they were thoroughly worried. My elderly dad had even researched all about online dating scams and was particularly concerned. Nonetheless, I persisted.

Irina lived with her parents in Omsk, Russia, in Siberia, and had never been on an airplane or driven a car. She had only been out of Russia once. She was well educated with degrees in nursing and accounting and, at the time, was a manager at her brother-in-law's bread factory. She also raised and showed champion poodles.

Irina's first flight ever was to Moscow to visit the French Embassy to get her five-day visa to Paris. A few weeks later, we were both on our way to Paris. I arrived first and remember waiting in Charles de Gaulle Airport thinking to myself, *This is really good, or this is really bad.* It was the first time I questioned what I was doing, or as some might say, "I had cold feet." What if Irina wasn't really who she had presented herself to be?

Once I saw Irina, though, she was more beautiful than her pictures, and we already knew so much about each other. We spent five beautiful days in Paris and I agreed to meet at her home in Russia after Christmas.

When I returned home, my family was relieved that I made it home safely. But they remained very skeptical of my approach to finding the right person to share my life with. They weren't alone in their skepticism. In early December, MarineMax had an awards cruise trip with many of our team as well as the board of directors. When I shared that I was headed to Siberia after Christmas and the reason why, I mostly received reactions like, "You're crazy," "That's a big risk," and "We're putting together a SWAT team to extract you!"

With all this negativity around me, I began questioning my decision. But then I thought about all the research I had done and the time I had invested and decided to head to Siberia. It was the right choice. I met Irina's family and had a wonderful time.

By now I knew I wanted to spend the rest of my life with Irina. We made plans to meet in January in Cortina, Italy, where a yacht manufacturer had arranged a snow ski trip. The Italian trip was great, plus Irina was able to meet my son, Brett, and daughter-in-law. They were shocked when I told them we were engaged. They agreed Irina was a special woman but at first couldn't quite reconcile the fact she would be a stepmother younger than they were. Of course, though, they came around and also accepted that they would have stepsisters or stepbrothers younger than their own kids.

Nonetheless, again I pressed forward with my plan. More challenges lay ahead, including trying to get a fiancée visa for Irina. This was post-9/11 and Homeland Security was incredibly strict. We discovered that Irina didn't need a visa to travel to the Dominican Republic, so we met there several times. My older daughters joined us there, too, and gave Irina the thumbs-up.

But the battle wasn't over. This was June and the U.S. Embassy in Moscow said they couldn't give us a visa interview date until October. Also, I had been told that it was "useless" to try to get them to move the date up. But by now you know it's not my personality to sit around and wait.

Against the advice of my immigration lawyers, I wrote letters to the U.S. Embassy in Moscow to get the date moved up. I told the embassy my eighty-five-year-old mother had been diagnosed with pancreatic cancer and could not travel to meet Irina. Almost immediately, they moved the interview date to late June, and of course we were approved. We were married August 26. My once-skeptical dad gave Irina away with my mom, kids, and grandkids watching. (Irina's parents couldn't be there because of visa issues.) As it turned out, this was the last opportunity that my mother would have had to be able to be at our wedding due to health issues. Yes, I do believe in fate and destiny!

This is my very best story of how calculated risk-taking can lead to the perfect outcome through persistence, commitment, and relentless caring. As I mentioned earlier, Irina and I have been married more than eighteen years and have two beautiful young daughters. I only wish my mom had lived to see my two younger daughters with Irina.

A POWERFUL TOOL WHEN USED PROPERLY

Risk and entrepreneurship are intertwined too. Consider the accomplishment of one of the biggest entrepreneurs and risk-takers in my lifetime, Elon Musk. From X.com (which became PayPal) to Tesla and Space X, Musk has tackled challenges that most people considered too big a gamble to even attempt.

I have owned six Tesla vehicles. With the first, I liked the idea and decided to risk trying something new. Fast-forward more than a decade later, and my wife and I are passionate about Tesla vehicles and their reliability, performance, and ownership experience. Musk took on the big auto manufacturers and changed the game.

Says Musk, "If something is important enough, you should try, even if the probable outcome is failure."[5]

Those wise words apply not only to what Musk has done for electric vehicles and batteries. He also took on the colossal (and what most thought to be insurmountable) challenge of running a private company that builds rockets with the goal of ferrying people and objects to space, the moon, Mars, and beyond.

Today SpaceX is flying high, ferrying government and private payloads into orbit at a fraction of what NASA and others charge even with recent inflation-sparked price increases.[6] Musk has gone beyond that, again doing what many people thought was impossible. His company lands spent rocket boosters on floating barges or land to be reused.

Taking risks for Musk is part of his DNA. Like him or not, he is changing the thinking around what is possible. What he has accomplished was extremely difficult, carried huge risks, and required a lot of hard work. But he exemplifies the idea that we can and must find opportunity amid difficulty. Indications are that even though Musk is one of the wealthiest people on the planet, he has only begun!

A DIFFERENT APPROACH

Author and growth expert Sujan Patel suggests certain entrepreneurial behaviors that align with risk-taking include:

- Looking at decisions from a reward-perspective, not from a risk-perspective
- Thinking outside the box to create solutions
- Viewing challenges optimistically—as opportunities, not problems
- Setting goals and having a vision for what you want to accomplish[7]

About a dozen years ago, a MarineMax executive, Steve Michael, and I were on a flight from Los Angeles to Atlanta when a fellow passenger told us that his scientists could make hydrogen from saltwater in a lab without using electrolysis. (Electrolysis is a process that uses electricity to separate the molecules of hydrogen and oxygen from ordinary water.)

Based on traditional science, what this Tucson, Arizona, company supposedly was doing seemed impossible. But, before someone rolls their eyes and turns away, remember that at one time almost everyone thought the world was flat, and we all know how that belief fizzled.

Such a process to produce hydrogen could be a crucial breakthrough in the quest for a more cost-effective green alternative to fossil fuels for power generation. So, with the idea that this could be a potential investment opportunity, Steve and I decided to risk a few days of our time to explore the possibility further and headed to Tucson.

Once there, we saw that the company was really doing what it claimed in a process that I believe has the potential to change the world, energy-wise. We did our research, and we invested our capital. Time will tell if the financial risks associated with investing in the process reap rewards. But without taking the risk, there can be no rewards.

A NOTE ABOUT RESEARCH

The wild card when it comes to risk is your research. Some is well done and some isn't. That sounds a bit like Research 101, but plenty of business (and personal) decisions are made every day without solid research to back them up.

The key is knowing how and where to find information and understanding how to identify biases. That way, you have as clear and honest an assessment of the pros and cons of a risk as possible.

Research often starts out online but should go well beyond that. If it's a product or service you're researching, standard operating procedure should include stepping into the consumer's shoes. If possible, experience whatever you're researching. Think about the catamaran charter trip that opened our eyes to the possibilities for excellence in customer experience.

With so much information a click or a voice command away today, it's easy to only get the information you want to hear instead of all that you *need* to hear. Beware, too, of one of the biggest mistakes people make in their research: distorting the research to validate a predetermined hypothesis. Political polls conducted by a particular group that poll mostly the organization's supporters are a prime example of that.

Pay attention to the sources of your information. Conjecture or opinion from individuals or organizations that are not qualified to provide an educated assessment are not reliable, accurate sources.

Many Sources

Hone your skills at information-gathering by taking the time to check out many different sources and consider lots of options. Research takes many forms, from talking to fellow team members and industry experts to reading publications and more. I like to do my initial research independent of fellow team members and then validate or brainstorm with others after that.

All this is time-consuming, but relatively straightforward with the help of a computer. Read and listen to what others say, and then draw your own conclusions. Too often, people only find one or two sources of information and then consider themselves experts on a topic. The solution then becomes their way or no way. Not helpful.

Take something as simple as information on the risks associated with a particular drug or medical procedure. Relying only on what the drug manufacturer says or what the medical provider says about the procedure means you haven't done enough research to make an educated decision. The drugmaker wants you to buy the drug and the medical provider wants to sell you the procedure. They may even get a kickback for recommending it.

No matter the topic or the challenge, though, listen to what others say. But make sure those others aren't just disgruntled or disappointed former employees taking to the internet to vent frustrations.

Research is such a simple solution to a pervasive problem in business and in life. We just must work hard to make sure to base our decisions on accurate and unbiased views.

And be honest with yourself when it comes to measuring the positives and negatives of success or failure. The positives must outweigh the negatives. Have a plan B in place, too, if the risk of plan A not working out could cause big problems.

Know Your Strengths and Weaknesses

I mentioned this earlier, but it's worth repeating because so many people ignore it: doing quality research also means recognizing and understanding your shortcomings. As a leader, it's what you don't know that makes a difference. Before we jumped on a plane and headed to Tucson, I thoroughly checked out the people and their credentials, the processes involved with extracting hydrogen from water, and more.

When I wanted MarineMax to get into the catamaran business, I knew catamarans weren't my specialty, so I found the best expert on catamaran building and the business that I could—Lex Raas—and brought him and his team in to help us study the markets. As a result, when we did enter the market, we thoroughly understood how to do just that. Even then it took hard work and perseverance to be successful. Can you imagine what would have happened if we went into the market without that kind of preparation? Suffice it to say, we likely would not be as successful as we are today or have been as successful as quickly.

Another example of knowing your strengths is what happened in 1997. When we were creating MarineMax and were preparing for the IPO, I convinced top financial expert Mike McLamb to join us as CFO. Together, we took the risks of executing the IPO and, for the past twenty-five years, we have thrived with McLamb as an A-plus CFO who embodies our values and cares for our team and their families.

DITCH THE EMOTIONS

Also, accept that not all ideas work. Sometimes pulling the plug on those ideas and the approaches that come up short is made more difficult than it has to be because leaders allow their emotions to become too intertwined in decision-making.

When it comes to assessing risk in business, leave the emotions out of the research. Relentlessly care, but be realistic and honest in your investigating. Then, with accurate pros and cons about something in mind, you can make your decision without emotion and take the necessary actions.

That may sound a bit contradictory—care, but leave the emotions out—but it's not. It's about making a decision based on an accurate big picture for all involved.

Let's say, for example, a leader has a friend who is a team member, yet, despite extensive coaching, that person is seriously underperforming in their role. That's a tough but all too common dilemma many leaders face. Does truly caring look like maintaining the friendship despite the low job performance, or is it about helping the team member succeed in a job or career through another position in the organization or finding a new employer?

Most of the time, the answer is the latter, but those actions are easier to take if your company's culture is one of clarity, communication, and relentless caring. MarineMax had a longtime loyal team member in its finance and insurance department. The individual was very successful at dealing with customers and banks, but then, as often happens, was promoted to a managerial position where they struggled.

Because of the transparency in our culture, friendship and loyalty were not a part of the leader's decision to move the individual back to a nonmanagerial role. Both sides understood the issues and the shortcomings. The solution / course of action became a no-brainer for all involved, and the individual is happily back in a role they enjoy. Once again, an organization's culture was the differentiator that made a decision simple and clear.

ASSESS YOUR LEADERSHIP: RISK ASSESSMENT

Do:

- Check out lots of different sources.
- Pay attention to the source of any information.
- Consider the biases of a source.
- Consider your own ingrained biases, both conscious and subconscious.
- When it comes to risk, leave your emotions out of the research.
- Admit your shortcomings.
- Relentlessly care.

Don't:

- Rely only on what your friends or colleagues say.
- Make a big decision without first thoroughly researching the risks.
- Expect success without hard work and research.
- Be afraid to ask questions and seek answers from multiple sources.
- Assume you know all there is to know.

TAKEAWAYS

- Risk is essential.
- Risk is the courage to step out of your comfort zone and reach higher.
- Thorough research is essential before taking a risk.
- The amount of risk someone is willing to accept is an individual choice and depends on the people around them, their research, and their commitment to a goal. That's true in business as well as our personal lives.
- The right kind of research is unbiased, in-depth, and accurate.
- Pay attention to the source of the information and potential biases that come with it.
- Know your strengths and weaknesses and be willing to tap into and learn from the experts.
- Quality research also means recognizing and understanding your shortcomings. As a leader, it's what you don't know that makes a difference.
- One of the biggest mistakes people make is to give in to the tendency to distort their research to validate a predetermined hypothesis.
- Another common mistake is doing too little research and using sources that are too similar.
- Leave your emotions out of your research, though emotions can enter into a final decision as long as you have considered all the pros and cons.

Addendum: How to Create a *Great* Health Insurance Plan for Your Teams

If you and/or your company truly want to deliver better quality, less expensive healthcare to your people, congratulations are in order. You are well on your way to embracing relentless caring as a way of life and doing business in a way that pays back dividends year after year.

Great health insurance is a gift to your teams. Some of its benefits include:

- high quality
- affordability for team members and employers
- steady rates
- no cost increases to team members
- declining cost to employer
- minimal or no co-pays
- dependability

- broad coverage
- minimal exclusions
- 24/7 access
- quick response times
- broad provider networks
- virtual care as much as possible
- use of centers of excellence as much as possible
- vetted, high-quality physicians and facilities
- ongoing mental health services
- caregiver support services (eldercare, childcare, pet care)
- financial well-being support services
- intensive oncology nurse support for cancer patients
- diabetes management care and ongoing consultation
- specialty drug programs at zero cost to the employee
- stem cell treatment options prior to orthopedic surgery

Whew! Not many organizations and certainly not many off-the-shelf insurance plans measure up to all that and more. The MarineMax self-insured health plan is one that does.

With self-insured plans, instead of an organization paying a third party huge sums to participate in and administer a prepackaged health plan, the organization contracts directly with vendors and networks of vendors to administer and operate its own plan. In other words, the traditional option is a one-stop shop with high costs/prices and limited alternatives. Self-insured plans involve creating your own network of the very best vendors, likely with big cost savings to everyone.

Our company loves it and team members do too. Don't take my word for it. Listen to what others say:

- "Before this new plan, every year our premiums increased. Now, the premiums have remained the same and the deductibles have dropped every year."
- "I had to take an expensive special drug—$1,400 per month—and our healthcare plan picked up the entire cost."
- "I needed shoulder surgery. Our out-of-pocket costs were Z-E-R-O."
- "What's covered under our health insurance plan? Check out our thirty-page benefits guide. Want to harvest and store umbilical cord blood? No problem. Need fertility treatments or plasma treatments? No problem there either. Physical therapy? Virtual visit? Alternative therapies? Mental healthcare? All are covered under our plan. That's something we never had with our old plan."
- "This new and different approach to health insurance coverage for our team members required a lot of work in the beginning, but now it's smooth sailing and we all benefit."

In 2015, MarineMax had about 1,200 employees and provided healthcare coverage for them under a traditional big insurance company plan at a cost of $10 million annually—and that doesn't include individual costs to team members. In 2021, with more than double the number of employees, MarineMax spent just $9 million on healthcare coverage through its self-insured health plan, MAXHealthPlan Solutions.

Ray Bowman, MarineMax senior vice president for talent and team development and the man who helped us make this shift, regularly talks to and works with companies to help them build their own self-insured plans at no charge to the companies. MarineMax does this as a public service to others. Ray recounts a personal experience from a number of years ago that was in part a catalyst that prompted him to create and develop this revolutionary approach. At the time, his insurance coverage was through one of the country's major health insurance plans. Back then, Ray had a procedure that he was told would cost $900. When his health insurer sent him an explanation of benefits, the plan had paid his doctor $9,000 for the procedure. It turned out the doctor's office had made a mistake on the claim and added an extra zero. But the insurance company never caught the error because the total amount paid was well within the dollar amount the plan would pay for the procedure—up to $20,000.

This is indicative of how broken the old, costly system was and is, and why companies may want to consider self-insurance alternatives, especially if saving money is important. Insurance companies pay little attention; they just write the checks, says Ray, and their clients—people and organizations that use them—pay the financial price. "We at MarineMax decided to take the time to pay attention, to do the due diligence, to partner with the right administrators, and to provide our teams with the best possible and affordable healthcare plan."

Of course, as with most everything else, implementation and acceptance of this new and different self-insured approach to healthcare hasn't always been smooth sailing for MarineMax or our teams. But as is also the case with most everything else, with commitment, persistence, and relentless caring front and center, the tide eventually changed.

That said, keep in mind there is no shortcut and no silver bullet to create a great healthcare plan for your team. There's good news and bad news: The bad news is that a lot of work has to go into developing the right plan for your people up front. The good news is that once the plan and providers are in place, it gets better, takes less work, gives your teams more, and the savings can roll in for everyone.

Let's look closer at how any organization can develop and implement its own *great* health insurance plan.

TOP-DOWN COMMITMENT

For any organization looking for a new (and better) health insurance plan, the journey starts from the top—the C-suite. The idea to have a great healthcare plan can't just be a human resources–sponsored initiative. No matter the size of a company or the industry, the commitment and the leadership must emanate from the top down.

That means the CEO of an organization must be thoroughly committed to what they firmly believe will be the positive outcomes of a conversion to a new approach to healthcare coverage. That kind of relentless commitment doesn't just apply to healthcare; it extends to any kind of change in pursuit of excellence.

Remember in chapter three when I discovered the Topgrading approach to hiring right and Brad Smart wanted to interview me before he ever committed to working with MarineMax? That was because Brad needed to know for certain that, as CEO, I wasn't just talking about hiring better and looking to cherry-pick a few good ideas from his Topgrading approach. He needed to see that I was fully committed to implementing the entire process at MarineMax and to know that I was an A player and a strong leader too.

Everyone likes to complain about the high cost of healthcare, especially around the election period for health insurance. That's annually when your teams can choose various insurance options and your insurance broker visits, full of warnings about how much more it will cost your organization for next year's healthcare and insurance, how benefits going into the next year will be cut, and how team member premiums and co-pays will be hiked.

All that can change, though—and it will if an organization's CEO, CFO, and the directors of HR have the courage to usher in change and the stamina to make it happen.

Is your organization's leader or are you as the leader ready for that kind of a commitment? Do they or you have the courage to make changes? Leadership must be serious about wanting change for the better.

OVERCOMING FEAR

Humans don't like change, period, in whatever form it takes; that's a given.[1] And if it involves something as stressful as health insurance and healthcare today, the fear is likely magnified. Add in the fear of the unknown, and we're all but overwhelmed.

Those years ago when MarineMax decided to pursue a better way to insure our teams, we were scared too. Our insurance broker back then told us our attempt to self-insure wouldn't work. He even went out of his way to promise that he would "take us back" when our plan failed. But then that broker stood to lose a lot of money if we dumped his plan in favor of our own.

My biggest fear in the beginning of talk about self-insuring was that we would not be able to provide our teams with at least the same level of care and service as a big provider. But, as healthcare and insurance costs with that provider continued to soar for both our company and our people, we decided to take the risk. Thankfully, my fears were unfounded as we learned that self-insuring meant we could far surpass the previous level of care and service.

To help calm any fears prompted by the idea of self-insuring, let's add some perspective to the numbers. Consider who actually pays for your healthcare. It's not really the insurer; it's employers and team members, too, who pay into the insurance pot that reimburses providers for the procedures, the diagnoses, the consults, the drugs, and more.

As I mentioned earlier, at the time MarineMax decided to self-insure, the company was paying about $10 million annually to provide health insurance for its teams (and bolster the profits of the insurance company). That doesn't count all the co-pays and premiums those team members were paying. If you're self-employed and paying into a health insurance policy, those pricey premiums are what fund your treatments (and insurance company profits). So, perhaps there's not as much at risk as we imagine.

If an organization decides to self-insure, what's really at risk is the loss to the company that administered the prepackaged plan and negotiated with provider networks to arrange payments. Thinking of it in those terms makes the concept a bit more manageable.

ELEMENTS OF A PLAN

As mentioned, creating a self-insured plan requires that an organization assemble its own vendors to provide the services associated with health insurance. Doing that takes, first, a thorough analysis of what services your existing provider offers plus any additional services and options you would like to offer your team. The goal is to identify the services that are necessary as well as any additional options—and then find the very best vendor for each.

Here's the MarineMax list of services. It's extensive, but don't be scared off by its length and the idea of finding the right vendor for each. Remember, as an organization MarineMax didn't set out to simply self-insure and provide our teams with the same mediocre to average benefits. Our primary goal was to deliver to our people the very best possible, affordable healthcare coverage. Once the vendors are in place, too, they are there year after year unless there is a need for a change.

The MarineMax list includes:

- claims administrator
- pharmacy benefits management
- physical therapy
- telemedicine
- mental health services
- claims auditing
- surgery
- surgery auditing
- dermatology
- newborn umbilical cord stem cell capture and long-term storage
- routine yearly physicals
- vision coverage
- dental coverage
- financial wellness
- caregiver support
- overseas concierge surgeries
- specialty drugs
- advanced pharmacist consultants
- stem cell therapies
- imaging services
- home delivery services for ongoing medications
- lactation support

- early cancer detection service
- diabetes management program
- cardiac support and services

Your list can be endless depending on the benefits an organization would like to offer its people and the cost of each. Once again, don't be overwhelmed by the volume. There are organizations that can ease the selection process.

KEEPING A LID ON COSTS

Of course, no matter how much an organization wants to provide the very best care and services to its teams, money must figure into the equation. Stop-loss must be part of the planning too. An organization can't afford to hemorrhage cash uncontrollably, even if it is for a good cause.

So, when identifying the best vendors to meet an organization's needs, keep an accurate record of the projected costs for each. Then, as you work on creating your own plan, you can determine what is feasible financially and what isn't. It's worthwhile to keep a list of backup vendors, too, in case a favored vendor doesn't negotiate the right price or falls short in its performance.

MarineMax keeps a lid on its costs by auditing every claim. In this case auditing is expenses oversight, something big insurers tend not to examine as closely line by line. For example, if someone has surgery involving stainless steel screws, the big insurance company—the insurance money pot—might be charged $38,000 for the packet of screws even though the actual operation only involved two screws. MarineMax pays for only the two screws. (And that's not a made-up example; this happens all the time with the traditional health insurance system.)

Or Ray offers an example of an actual prescriptions audit: one patient was prescribed a new and very expensive stomach medicine that turned out to be no more than a combination of two familiar and easily available and affordable drugs.

All this auditing isn't about administrators or nonmedical people meddling in someone's medical care. This is oversight by people who relentlessly care about others and want them to get the best possible quality and fairest care and treatments available.

Some things to consider when selecting a vendor include:

1. Start by evaluating what you need to add to your program. Where are the pain points, where are your employees suffering most, and where are the biggest spending areas for your plan?
2. Spend the time necessary to look at several vendor options. Ask for and contact numerous references and ask for specific outcomes data. In other words, look at the facts.
3. Do cost projections and savings projections.
4. Don't sign lengthy contracts. Demand a one-year or shorter agreement so that you can "test-drive" what the vendor does and how your employees really benefit. Also always include a thirty-day escape clause in case you need to break ties with a vendor earlier than the trial period.

For example, with the last point, in spite of MarineMax identifying what we thought was a good dental plan, after implementation it became clear that some aspects of the plan could be improved. We were open to continuing to shop for more extensive dental coverage and especially a rollover of unused dollars into the next fiscal year.

Don't be afraid to continue to tweak your benefits plan until you're satisfied that your employees are accessing the very best benefit available. That's just one more part of the commitment to relentless caring and excellence we expect.

RELENTLESS PERSISTENCE

Refusing to give up in the wake of challenges is another part of that commitment to excellence. MarineMax moved to an open-provider approach to healthcare because we thought it was the best possible option for our team members. An open approach means anyone can go to any provider they choose; someone doesn't have to be "in-network." Sounds simple enough, right? Wrong!

Over and over our employees were told by the doctors' offices that they were "out of network." The receptionists in many doctors' offices did not understand the concept of an open network; even when it was explained to them, they didn't believe it—they couldn't believe it. It was one of those "too good to be true" premises. Nonetheless, we persisted and engaged the largest network of physicians in the United States.

Keep in mind, too, that a health plan literally is like a living being. You always need to be prepared to make adjustments and improvements as things change and needs arise over time. Again, it's back to the MarineMax relentless commitment to put together the most vibrant, strongest, and most beneficial health plan possible for the sake of our employees and our companies. That's relentless caring.

SENSITIVE TO THE NEEDS OF YOUR PEOPLE

The early implementation of the MarineMax self-insured plan wasn't easy for our people or for our organization. That's an expected part of implementing change of any kind.

We had to work with our vendors to get it right; we switched a few vendors too. Team members struggled to find providers, even though ours was that "open plan" where any doctor anywhere will receive reimbursement. One of the challenges with such an unlimited plan is that most people—patients and providers—are accustomed to working with "provider networks" where, if a provider is outside of a network, the out-of-pocket cost for services is higher. That wasn't the case with our plan, but because it was different, some people—especially providers—had trouble understanding that. In fact, that has been an ongoing issue to the point that only recently we had to switch to a specific broad provider network instead.

A health plan must be changeable, as mentioned earlier. One day the MarineMax HR department received a telephone call concerning a team member's seven-year-old daughter who had just been diagnosed with type 1 diabetes. Her father was a blue-collar yard worker, and although he was paid well compared with others in his position elsewhere, the family simply could not afford to pay for their daughter's very expensive medications like insulin.

On the spot, that same day, MarineMax decided to make changes. We couldn't allow someone to have to go without their required medications, so we changed our health plan. Now, if an employee or their family member has diabetes and agrees to participate in our diabetes management program, where they receive individualized help to control their condition, we pay for all of their medication. This is a great illustration of how being in charge of your health plan (versus having a large insurance company package) can make a huge difference in the quality of life for your employees.

SANDBOX ROLLOUT

One of the lessons I learned from implementing our plan, too, is that, in retrospect, a limited, sandbox-type rollout could be advantageous for an organization. If, for example, a company has divisions or multiple stores, you may want to consider launching your plan on a small scale—perhaps in one store or one division—first. Then it's easier to identify and rectify the weaknesses and challenges before a company-wide launch.

An added benefit of a sandbox rollout is the development of champions—those team members who can then promote and share the advantages of the new approach with fellow team members. That can make company-wide rollout and acceptance easier.

Here's an additional thought to keep in mind when a company and its leaders are considering whether to change and upgrade the health insurance for their teams: If you choose not to make this change or, at the very least, learn more about what MarineMax has done and the benefits our team enjoys, please take some time to soul-search. Ask yourself why you are opting to remain with the old, expensive, limited health plan you now have. Think hard and clearly about why you want to avoid change and improvement. Are you simply looking for excuses?

Lethargy is an enemy and it is you, your own family, and the families of all of your team members that will needlessly suffer from your fear.

MY GIFT TO YOU

If you or your organization—large, small, or somewhere in between—are interested in learning more about MarineMax's MAXHealthPlan Solutions (MHS) strategy and how to put together a great healthcare insurance system for your teams, visit http://MaxHealthPlanSolutions.com. The information is free of charge, no strings attached. You can also contact Ray Bowman, PhD, president of MHS, at MHSPlan@MarineMax.com.

Where to Go for More Information

Some Good Reads

Start with Why: How Great Leaders Inspire Everyone to Take Action by Simon Sinek

The Go-Giver: A Little Story About a Powerful Business Idea by Bob Burg and John David Mann

Go-Givers Sell More by Bob Burg and John David Mann

Topgrading by Bradford D. Smart, PhD

Foolproof Hiring: Powerful, Fully Proven Keys to Hiring HIGH Performers by Brad Smart and Chris Mursau

The Ultimate Question by the Bain Corporation

Winning on Purpose: The Unbeatable Strategy of Loving Customers by Fred Reichheld

Elon Musk: Tesla, SpaceX, and the Quest for a Fantastic Future by Ashlee Vance

Other Resources

Topgrading.com
MarineMax.com
Simon Sinek:

- TedTalk: "Start with Why," www.youtube.com/watch?v=2Ss78LfY3nE
- TedTalk: "How to Discover Your Why in Difficult Times," www.ted.com/talks/simon_sinek_how_to_discover_your_why_in_difficult_times?language=en
- The Optimism Library, simonsinek.com/the-optimism-library/

Acknowledgments

So many individuals have contributed so much to help me on my journey to where I am today. To each of you, a sincere and heartfelt thank-you for your teaching, guidance, advice, help, and inspiration.

Notes

CHAPTER 1

1. Marcel Schwantes, "Why Are People Quitting Their Jobs? It May Come Down to One Thing They're Not Getting from Employers," *Inc.*, February 12, 2022, https://www.inc.com/marcel-schwantes/why-are-people-quitting-their-jobs-it-may-come-down-to-1-thing-theyre-not-getting-from-employers.html.
2. Sigal Barsade and Olivia A. O'Neill, *Harvard Business Review*, "Employees Who Feel Love Perform Better," January 13, 2014, https://hbr.org/2014/01/employees-who-feel-love-perform-better.
3. Randstad, "Businesses Need to Step Up, as Millennials and Gen Z Fundamentally Change the Employer-Employee Power Dynamic—Global Survey of 35,000 Workers," April 4, 2022, https://tools.eurolandir.com/tools/Pressreleases/GetPressRelease/?ID=4082017&lang=en-GB&companycode=nl-rand&v=.
4. Ibid.

CHAPTER 2

1. ITA Group, "Eight Ways to Increase Customer Lifetime Value," 2021 white paper, https://info.itagroup.com/rs/614-FWE-386/images/ita-group-white-paper-8-ways-to-increase-customer-lifetime-value.pdf.
2. Yahoo! Finance, "Marine Max, Inc.," Historical Data, https://finance.yahoo.com/quote/HZO/history.

CHAPTER 3

1. CareerBuilder, "Nearly Three in Four Employers Affected by a Bad Hire, According to a Recent CareeerBuilder Survey," December 7, 2017, press release, https://press.careerbuilder.com/2017-12-07-Nearly-Three-in-Four-Employers-Affected-by-a-Bad-Hire-According-to-a-Recent-CareerBuilder-Survey.
2. Topgrading Inc., "A Practical Definition of 'A Player,'" (blog), November 18, 2021, https://topgrading.com/resources/blog/a-practical-definition-of-a-player.
3. Ibid.
4. Nayeli Nomeli, "Fact Check: No, Albert Einstein Did Not Say Famous Quote About Fish Climbing Trees," *USA TODAY*, April 27, 2021, http://www.usatoday.com/story/news/factcheck/2021/04/27/fact-check-einstein-never-said-quote-fish-climbing-trees/7384370002.
5. John Sullivan, "Ouch, 50% of New Hires Fail! Six Ugly Numbers Revealing Recruiting's Dirty Little Secret," ERE Recruiting Intelligence, April 10, 2017, http://www.ere.net/ouch-50-of-new-hires-fail-6-ugly-numbers-revealing-recruitings-dirty-little-secret/.
6. The Evolving Enterprise, "Over 50% of All Hires Fail, New Survey Reveals," (blog), June 24, 2021, http://www.theee.ai/2021/06/24/11021-over-50-of-all-sales-hires-fail-new-survey-reveals.
7. Northwestern University Human Resources, "The Cost of a Bad Hire," Northwestern University, accessed November 21, 2022, http://www.northwestern.edu/hr/about/news/february-2019/the-cost-of-a-bad-hire.html.
8. Bradford D. Smart, *Topgrading: How Leading Companies Win by Hiring, Coaching, and Keeping the Best People* (New York: Portfolio/Penguin Group, 2005), 44.
9. Lisa Frye, "The Cost of a Bad Hire Can Be Astronomical," SHRM, May 9, 2017, https://www.shrm.org/resourcesandtools/hr-topics/employee-relations/pages/cost-of-bad-hires.aspx.
10. Topgrading Inc., "The High Costs of Mis-Hires Are Higher Than You Think," (blog), June 25, 2019, https://topgrading.com/resources/blog/the-high-costs-of-mis-hires-are-higher-than-you-think.
11. Talogy, "About Caliper: Founders Story," accessed November 7, 2022, https://calipercorp.com/about-caliper.
12. Ibid.
13. Bradford D. Smart, email interviews by Susan J. Marks, October 31, 2022, January 20, 2023.
14. Smart, *Topgrading*, 36–37.
15. Topgrading Inc., "General Electric Case Study (1987–2000)," Topgrading Inc. web

page, October 31, 2022, https://topgrading.com/resources/case-studies/general-electric/.

16. Smart, email interviews by Susan J. Marks.
17. Luisa Zhou, "The Ultimate List of Life Coaching Statistics in 2023," (blog), January 2, 2023, https://www.luisazhou.com/blog/life-coaching-statistics.
18. Claire Hastwell, "Creating a Culture of Recognition," (blog), September 9, 2021, https://www.greatplacetowork.com/resources/blog/creating-a-culture-of-recognition.
19. Ibid.
20. Great Place To Work, "Trust Model: Leading the Way For All™ Methodology," Great Place To Work web page, November 18, 2022, https://www.greatplacetowork.com/our-methodology.
21. Mark Sherman, "As Others See Us: Others May See Us Doing Far Better Than We Think We Are," (blog), December 4, 2013, https://www.psychologytoday.com/us/blog/real-men-dont-write-blogs/201312/others-see-us.
22. Caitlin Mazur, "20 Essential Employee Feedback Statistics (2023): Employees Want More Than Just Performance Reviews," Zippia.com, February 1, 2023, https://www.zippia.com/advice/employee-feedback-statistics.
23. Steelcase, "The New Era of Hybrid Work: It's Time to Give People What They Want," February 2022, https://www.steelcase.com/content/uploads/2022/03/2022_SC_Global Report_Final.pdf.

CHAPTER 5

1. "The Easy Prey Podcast Hosted by Chris Parker: How to Spot a Liar with Pamela Meyer," YouTube video, accessed November 8, 2022, https://www.youtube.com/watch?v=jB09sgg0NCk.
2. Jack Welch, "Over-Delivering in Your Career," YouTube video, Jack Welch Management Institute, posted by Pavan CH, Human Engineers, https://humanengineers.com/over-delivering-in-your-career.
3. Jostle in Social Software in the Workplace, "Jostle People Engagement Platform Alternatives," Gartner, https://www.gartner.com/reviews/market/workplace-social-software/vendor/jostle/product/jostle-people-engagement-platform/alternatives.
4. Theodore Roosevelt, "Believe You Can," Theodore Roosevelt Center at Dickinson State University, accessed November 30, 2022, https://www.theodorerooseveltcenter.org/Search?r=1&searchTerms=believe%20you%20can&f=Quotes&ro=1&pl=1&cp=1.
5. Rose Kennedy, "44+ Best Quotes from Rose Kennedy, Exclusive Selection," BayArt: New Perspective on Life, accessed November 30, 2022, https://bayart.org/rose-kennedy-quotes.

6. Renu Khator, "Fall Address," University of Houston press release, October 3, 2012, https://www.uh.edu/president/newsroom/pdf-files/Fall-Address-2012-Script.pdf.
7. Marc Antonius, "Lessons from a Guy Who Sold More Than 120 Million Albums," *Spread Your Talent* (blog), February 18, 2014, https://spreadyourtalent.com/blog/lessons-from-a-guy-who-sold-more-than-120-million-albums.
8. Lou Holtz, "Do Right: Doing Right (1988)," YouTube video, posted by Real Life Training Films, April 16, 2014, https://www.youtube.com/watch?v=lrL5qvGWArw.
9. Walt Disney / Disney Careers, accessed October 12, 2022, https://mobile.twitter.com/disneycareers/status/958006828104904707; "Keep Moving Forward," YouTube video, posted by Darren Wittko, March 18, 2014, https://www.youtube.com/watch?v=RRFDgDeboqE.
10. National Museum of American History, "Never Doubt That a Small Group of Thoughtful Committed Citizens Can Change the World: Indeed It's the Only Thing That Ever Has. Margaret Mead," Smithsonian, https://americanhistory.si.edu/collections/search/object/nmah_1285394.
11. All American Entertainment, "Carol Dweck, the Power of Mindset and Psychology of Success," June 29, 2017, https://www.allamericanspeakers.com/blog/carol-dweck-mindsets.
12. TED, "Our Mission: Spread Ideas, Foster Community, and Create Impact," accessed November 7, 2022, https://www.ted.com/about/our-organization.
13. Amazon.com, "Help Make History Starting with Day 1," accessed April 19, 2023, https://www.amazon.jobs/en/landing_pages/:~:text=Amazon's%20mission%20is%20%22to%20be,the%20heart%20of%20that%20mission.
14. Microsoft, "About," accessed November 12, 2022, https://www.microsoft.com/en-us/about.
15. OpenAI, "OpenAI Is an AI Research and Deployment Company. Our Mission Is to Ensure That Artificial General Intelligence Benefits All of Humanity," accessed November 3, 2022, https://openai.com/about.
16. Google, "Our Mission Is to Organize the World's Information and Make It Universally Accessible and Useful," accessed November 3, 2022, https://about.google/?fg=1&utm_source=google-US&utm_medium=referral&utm_campaign=hp-header.

CHAPTER 6

1. Darren Overfield and Rob Kaiser, "One Out of Every Two Managers Is Terrible at Accountability," *Harvard Business Review*, November 8, 2012, https://hbr.org/2012/11/one-out-of-every-two-managers-is-terrible-at-accountability.
2. Grigore, "What Is a Good Net Promoter Score? 2022 NPS Benchmark," *Retently* (blog), April 18, 2022, https://www.retently.com/blog/good-net-promoter-score.

CHAPTER 7

1. Amina Islam, "How to Deal with Rejection," *Thrive Global* (blog), August 2, 2017, https://medium.com/thrive-global/how-to-deal-with-rejection-49741124221.
2. Statista Research Department, "Number of Starbucks Stores Worldwide from 2003 to 2022," November 28, 2022, https://www.statista.com/statistics/266465/number-of-starbucks-stores-worldwide.
3. McDonald's, "Our History: The Ray Kroc Story," accessed November 28, 2022, https://www.mcdonalds.com/us/en-us/about-us/our-history.html.
4. Pat Crawford and Wendy Fink, "From Academia to the Workforce: Navigating Persistence, Ambiguity, Change, and Conflict in the Workplace," Association of Public & Land Grant Universities Series on Employability Skills in Agriculture and Natural Resources, 2020, p. 11, accessed November 10, 2022, https://www.aplu.org/library/from-academia-to-the-workforce-navigating-persistence-ambiguity-change-and-conflict-in-the-workplace/file.
5. Jim Rohn, Twitter post, September 7, 2014, 8:30 PM, https://twitter.com/officialjimrohn/status/508804420025745408.
6. Oxford Learners Dictionaries, Oxford University Press, 2023, accessed November 12, 2022, https://www.oxfordlearnersdictionaries.com/definition/english/persistent#:~:text=%2Fp%C9%99%CB%88s%C9%AAst%C9%99nt%2F,are%20being%20annoying%20or%20unreasonable.
7. Stephanie Vozza, "How to Be Persistent at Work Without Being Obnoxious," *Fast Company* (blog), October 10, 2019, https://www.fastcompany.com/90414836/how-to-be-persistent-at-work-without-being-obnoxious.
8. Julian Birkinshaw and Jordan Cohen, "Make Time for the Work That Matters," *Harvard Business Review*, September 2013, https://hbr.org/2013/09/make-time-for-the-work-that-matters.

CHAPTER 8

1. Rachel Spencer, "How the Space Race Built Today's Technology," *Alliance for Innovation and Infrastructure* (blog), July 8, 2021, https://www.aii.org/how-the-space-race-built-todays-technology/.
2. Rebecca White, email interview by Susan J. Marks, June 2, 2022.
3. Albert Einstein, "Albert Einstein Quotes," DictionaryBook, accessed September 12, 2022, https://www.dictionarybook.org/quotes/albert-einstein.html.
4. Richard R. Riker and Giles L. Fraser, "In the Middle of Difficulty Lies Opportunity—Albert Einstein," *Critical Care Medicine* 46 (November 2018): 1881–1882. DOI: 10.1097/CCM.0000000000003399.

5. Elon Musk, Twitter post, December 1, 2016, 8 PM, https://twitter.com/elonmusk newsorg/status/804520587725045760?lang=en.
6. Victor Tangermann, "Elon Musk: SpaceX Launches Will Cost 1% of Current NASA Launches: Can Musk's Latest Claim Possibly Be True?" *Futurism*, November 6, 2019, https://futurism.com/spacex-launch-cost-less-nasa; Mike Wall, "SpaceX Raises Launch and Starlink Prices Citing Inflation," Space.com, March 23, 2022, https://www.space.com/spacex-raises-prices-launch-starlink-inflation.
7. Wharton Online / Wharton University of Pennsylvania, "Is Risk-Taking Behavior Key to Entrepreneurial Spirit?" (blog), February 4, 2020, https://online.wharton.upenn.edu/blog/is-risk-taking-behavior-key-to-entrepreneurial-spirit/#:~:text=Risk%2Dtaking%20enables%20and%20encourages,eventually%20lead%20to%20business%20growth.

ADDENDUM

1. Gustavo Razzetti, "How to Overcome the Fear of Change," *Psychology Today* (blog), September 18, 2018, https://www.psychologytoday.com/us/blog/the-adaptive-mind/201809/how-overcome-the-fear-change.

About the Author

William "Bill" H. McGill Jr. is the ideal person to share what it takes to be a successful leader in today's tough business world. He's the cofounder, former CEO (for twenty-two years), and now executive chairman of the board of MarineMax, the world's largest recreational boat and yacht retailer. Bill doesn't just talk about relentless kindness; he lives it 24/7. Many of those same individuals who launched MarineMax on the floor of the New York Stock Exchange in June 1998 were still there to celebrate its twentieth anniversary. That's a testament to a company's strong leadership and the strong culture of caring that Bill relentlessly fosters in all that he does and his teams do.

Bill knows what it takes to pursue your passions and have fun doing it. Born and raised on a farm in Tennessee, he's a mechanical engineer by formal training. He began his career as a test engineer for Pratt & Whitney Aircraft, designing and developing jet engines for the SR-71 spy plane. He moved on to work at Northrop Nortronics as a subcontractor for NASA and was involved in the early space station program systems. His dream and passion at the time was to be among the first astronauts at the space station. Those aspirations, though, changed when the funding for the U.S. space program stalled.

With the realization that it would be years before the United States focused on the space station, Bill decided to apply his engineering, leadership, and management skills elsewhere: manufacturing engineering at the Kendall Company. Several years later, not long after Kendall was sold to Colgate-Palmolive, the company wanted to transfer him to the Northeast—the choice was Boston or New York City. An avid and passionate water-skier, Bill decided that the cold winters in the suburbs of a major metropolitan area weren't where he and his wife wanted to raise their three kids. So, with his passion at the forefront, he invested his life savings into being a partner in his uncle's Sarasota, Florida–based retail boat business, and opened a branch in St. Petersburg—Gulfwind Marine.

As is typical with so many entrepreneurs—and often business leaders in general—Bill knew little about hiring, retaining, or promoting. But he did understand the importance of people and letting them know he genuinely cared about them and their families. That approach to leadership combined with hard work resulted in marine retailing history.

Those first years were tough: an energy crisis gripping the nation was followed by various recessions, each with its own challenges. But Bill was able to expand the business into multiple boat dealerships along Florida's west coast. Then, with the idea to change the fragmented marine industry, Bill and four other boat dealerships joined forces and, through an IPO in 1998, created MarineMax, a NYSE-listed company (HZO).

Today the company sells new and used boats (from eleven-foot boats to yachts over two hundred feet) and related marine products and services. MarineMax owns and operates yacht brokerage companies and charter businesses, manufactures boats and yachts, provides finance and insurance services through wholly owned subsidiaries, owns and operates marinas worldwide, and operates MarineMax Vacations in Tortola (in the British Virgin Islands) and the Bahamas. The company also operates Boatyard, a pioneering digital platform that enhances the boating experience.

More importantly, with Bill's guidance, MarineMax has established an unparalleled standard of customer care and service in the typically fragmented, often struggling retail boating industry. "We change people's lives" is the MarineMax mantra, and Bill and MarineMax's almost four thousand team members live that mantra to the fullest.

It's not that everything Bill does works, or that whatever he's involved in is a success. Rather, it's that, even starting small as he did with Gulfwind Marine, Bill's relentless caring and kindness toward others, persistence, and attention to even the smallest details with team members set him apart in terms of his ability to understand people and what works in business and what doesn't. It's what creates his unique leadership style, which he shares in *Relentless Caring.*